PLYMOUTH
A CITY AT WAR
1914–45

PLYMOUTH
A CITY AT WAR
1914–45

John Van der Kiste

The
History
Press

Frontispiece: There are several war memorials in Plymouth: the largest is on Plymouth Hoe and commemorates the Royal Naval dead of the two world wars. (By kind permission of Matilda Richards)

First published 2014

The History Press
The Mill, Brimscombe Port
Stroud, Gloucestershire, GL5 2QG
www.thehistorypress.co.uk

British Library Cataloguing in Publication Data.
A catalogue record for this book is available from the British Library.

ISBN 978 0 7524 8965 0

Typesetting and origination by The History Press
Printed in Great Britain

CONTENTS

ACKNOWLEDGEMENTS

My greatest thanks are due to Derek Tait, who generously allowed me full use of his excellent collection of local history illustrations relating to Plymouth during the wars, as well as cheerfully aiding my research by answering a number of questions on related topics during the course of my research and writing. Steve Johnson of www.cyberheritage.co.uk has also generously permitted the use of several illustrations for the purpose. Chris Robinson has been extremely helpful with various queries and, as ever, Brian Moseley's online Encyclopedia of Plymouth History has been a never-ending source of information and facts. Without them it is doubtful whether this book would ever have been written; it is certainly much the better for their assistance.

I am also grateful to Matilda Richards, at The History Press, who originally suggested the project; and to my wife Kim, who read through the draft, for their unfailing help and support throughout; to Ruth Boyes for her work editing the text; to the staff at Plymouth and West Devon Record Office, for allowing access to and permission to quote archive material; and to the staff at Plymouth Library Services, Drake Circus, for their regular and unfailing assistance with access to relevant materials in print and on microfilm.

THE FIRST WORLD WAR

1

COUNTDOWN TO WAR

To some of those who lived in Plymouth, the call to arms on 4 August 1914 might have come like a bolt from the blue. However, for most of the military and naval authorities, as well as many politicians, it was the unhappy but inevitable outcome of several factors. Foremost among these was the evermore tangled network of primarily defensive treaties between one European nation and another, instability in south-east Europe, particularly the Balkan region, and above all the Anglo-German naval and arms race. By the beginning of the year, the mood was growing throughout the south-west region of England, as well as the country at large, that it would be more a case of when war should break out, rather than if. As summer wore on, it became increasingly inevitable.

There had been ominous portents for some time. In July 1904, one month after King Edward VII had visited Berlin and had been freely shown around the German navy, the German battle fleet had been invited on a three-day visit to Plymouth. Diplomatic niceties required a reciprocal event and, on 10 July, the people of the three towns of Plymouth, Devonport and Stonehouse came in their thousands to the Hoe and the seafront to watch a procession of German warships arriving in the Sound. They were witnesses to an event without precedent, for this was the largest and most powerful foreign naval force that had ever paid a friendly visit to a British port. Both sides were agreeable enough to each other on the surface as the guests were entertained with fitting receptions and banquets, but some observers were uneasy. After the German fleet had returned home, journalists and newspaper editors expressed grave concerns about such fraternisation. In parliament questions were asked: was the Admiralty aware that German naval officers had been seen taking photographs of the fortifications and dockyard, and if so, did anybody propose to take any action? Naturally nothing could be done, but it was a salutary warning that in future it would be as well to err on the side of caution when welcoming military or naval representatives of foreign powers.

Only a year earlier, the writer and aspiring Member of Parliament Erskine Childers had published *The Riddle of the Sands*, a very widely-read and influential novel which predicted an invasion by Germany on an ill-prepared Britain. In 1912 Childers was adopted as a prospective Liberal candidate for Devonport, although he resigned his candidacy shortly afterwards and never fought an election. He was executed for treason in 1922, during the Irish civil war.

By this time, Plymouth was taking important action to ensure that in the event of hostilities the south-west would be as well prepared as anywhere else in Britain. The three contiguous towns of Plymouth, Devonport and Stonehouse had expanded steadily throughout the nineteenth century, and a strong body of opinion maintained that they should unite as one. Plymouth authorities and ratepayers overwhelmingly favoured such a move, while the majority of those in Devonport relished their independence and were determined to retain it, and the much smaller Stonehouse seemed undecided. At an enquiry which opened in January 1914 at Plymouth Guildhall, an application was made by Plymouth Corporation for a provisional order for the amalgamation of the county boroughs of Plymouth and Devonport, and the urban district of East Stonehouse. The Corporation spokesmen stated that in all respects but their government they were as one. J.H. Ellis, the Town Clerk, and Major-General A.P. Penton, Commander of the South Western Coast Defences, both supported the application. The latter, who had been asked by the War Office to put forward the military point of view, said that in peacetime organisation of the three towns into three district bodies was of little importance, but in wartime it would be a different matter. In the event of an order for mobilisation, the fortress commander would have to deal with three different authorities instead of one. Given the ever-increasing German threat to European stability and the possibility that Britain might very soon be at war, this measure could not be postponed much longer.

A bill confirming the order was passed by a Select Committee of the House of Commons on 15 July. Throughout that same month, the defences at Plymouth Sound were rigorously tested, with searchlights at night illuminating ships at anchor. No vessel was allowed to enter by night or day without a permit, and those which attempted to do so were met with a hail of gunfire from the batteries. Mariners were forbidden to enter or leave harbour during night or in fog, and were ordered to keep well clear of ships belonging to the Royal Navy.

Although the German Empire began mobilisation on 30 July and France followed two days later, it was by no means inevitable that Great Britain would be drawn into the fray. Many people who did not expect war – and they could be readily forgiven – were caught unawares in the escalating timetable. One Plymouth woman, who had probably been unaware of the rapidly deteriorating situation or was perhaps reluctant to believe that the worst could happen, had gone on holiday to Paris and was advised to return as swiftly as possible. Caught up in the turmoil, she fought her way through the panic-stricken crowds that thronged the streets of the French capital to the railway station and, by sheer good fortune, managed to secure herself a place on the last available train to Calais. She then endured a four-hour journey in great discomfort before reaching the port and an equally fraught crossing to Dover before she was able to get back home.

Like a number of his colleagues in the military and naval authorities, Major Penton considered that forewarned was forearmed. For a few days he had appealed for gaps to be filled in the local territorial forces. Able-bodied men, encouraged by their employers, patriotically went to the recruiting stations, ready to do their duty for king and country and enlist. Civilians watched with curiosity if not increasing alarm as soldiers marched to the barracks in readiness, and men of the Royal Naval Reserve, many of them fishermen, reported for duty at the Exchange in Woolster Street. On 2 August, although it was a Sunday, streets in the town centre of Plymouth were full, and it was impossible to pass outside the newspaper offices, where telegrams advising of the latest in the international situation were placed on display within minutes of arrival. Sentries were posted at Government property and other strategically important buildings. Monday, 3 August was a Bank Holiday, but on the whole people were not in a holiday mood and few travelled any distance from home. Less people went on railway and steamboat excursions than usual, and some were cancelled through lack of demand. At the theatres, attendances were likewise considerably down. Crowds in the street stood anxiously waiting for news, while the sight of men in uniform became increasingly frequent, and the territorials were on standby if needed.

At 11.00 p.m. on 4 August, in the words attributed to the Foreign Secretary Sir Edward Grey, the lamps were going out all over Europe. Britain declared war on Germany, preparing to take up arms against another European country for the first time since the end of the Crimean War in 1856. The naval arms race, and the frenzied situation which had been accelerating throughout Europe since the assassination in Bosnia of the Austro-Hungarian heir Archduke Franz Ferdinand and his wife at Sarajevo on 28 June, had made conflict involving most of the continental powers almost inevitable.

An announcement was posted in the windows of the *Western Morning News* offices just before midnight. People were aware that the international situation was deteriorating, and a large group had gathered in anticipation of such an event. According to one of the paper's reporters at the scene, 'The news caused a profound sensation, several women swooning, and a long murmur of excitement passed through the crowd.' In those pre-radio broadcasting days, the fact that declaration had taken place so late at night meant that few others in Plymouth, apart from those with telephones who were in regular contact with people in London, knew anything about it until the following morning. Official war notices were placed in the newspaper office windows and displayed on placards, and further details were given in the press the next day.

Paranoia soon took hold, with people thinking they saw spies at every possible turn. Aliens and suspected aliens were rounded up, and anybody with a German name or even a German accent was particularly vulnerable. On the night of 4 August, three men of apparently suspicious character were arrested on the eastern side of Plymouth Sound as they tried to break through recently erected wire entanglements. They were presumably harmless civilians who were trying to find their way home, perhaps after an evening of conviviality, and released after questioning with a caution to be more careful in future. A Russian steamer sailing from New York which reached Plymouth Sound that week had several American passengers who were keen to return home and stay out of Europe at a time of war, in addition to Germans and Russians who likewise needed to get back so they could discharge their patriotic duties against each other.

Within twenty-four hours of the announcement, panic buying had begun. Grocers did particularly brisk business, with customers having to wait a long time to be served, and prices of foodstuffs in shops virtually under siege fluctuated from hour to hour according to how much was available. Those who could afford to ordered large quantities of goods, such as half tons of flour and sugar by the hundredweight, thus creating a shortage which drove up prices in the short term. Tradesmen and retailers found themselves having to ration supplies or reduce the size of orders from customers whom they considered were probably hoarding. The mayor appealed for people to show restraint, asking the well-to-do not to increase stocks of provisions and stores, in order to help ensure that there would be enough for everyone.

Strange though it may seem with hindsight, the declaration of hostilities was greeted with considerable excitement, even enthusiasm, throughout much of Britain, and Plymouth was no exception. An increase in dockyard activity was anticipated with more employment, more ships to be built and serviced, and therefore more wealth for the workforce. In 1914 the dockyard employed over 10,000 men, and by the time peace had been declared this figure had risen to almost 19,000. The workers were not to be disappointed as their wages were in effect doubled by war bonuses, and supplemented by generous amounts of overtime. Because of the shortage of manpower, large numbers of women were employed in the yard for the first time. Routine repair and maintenance work, repairing damaged ships and fitting out Q-ships in campaigns against the U-boats, meant there was never any shortage of work.

Even so, not everybody anticipated a long war, and there was a widespread view that it would all be over by Christmas. Enthusiasm and patriotic feelings ran high. Young men in Plymouth who were disenchanted with what they saw as a tedious life at home, with little if any prospect of excitement, rallied to the cause of king and country. Patriotic feelings, reinforced through generations of family life and a strict upbringing which imbued in them a deep respect for the established order and the British Empire, ran high. A few public meetings organised by socialist societies and the trade unions were called to protest against the war, but most of them had to contend with crowds drowning them out by heckling and singing 'Rule Britannia', as well as cheers for England, the Empire and the armed services. Conservative and Liberal party workers eagerly went out, canvassing houses door to door, in an effort to persuade able-bodied and eager young men to join the army.

In the judiciary, a county court judge said that, in order to avoid undue hardship to the working classes and in view of the national situation, he was prepared to modify orders which were being made against debtors. For some, this may have been cause for mild celebration. Organisers of regattas and other seasonal sporting events were less happy, for many of the events they had worked so hard to prepare were quickly cancelled.

2

THE EARLY DAYS
OF WAR

During the first few days, much of the movement of troops took place at night and went largely unnoticed by the public. Bands marched with them, but did not play, in order to avoid disturbing those who were sleeping in houses nearby. Local accommodation would soon prove a problem, with many naval recruits having difficulty in finding lodgings. Several hundred who were granted shore leave found that most of the pubs with bed and breakfast facilities near the barracks were closed or full up.

HMS *Amphion*, a Devonport-manned cruiser, was the first warship of the conflict to be sunk by enemy action, on 6 August 1914, while patrolling the North Sea route from Harwich to Antwerp.

It was not long before Plymouth would have the first of many severe losses to report. Within thirty-six hours HMS *Amphion* had been lost at sea. A Devonport-manned cruiser, she had been ordered to patrol the North Sea from Harwich to Antwerp to keep the sea lanes open. A German minelayer, *Königin Louise*, had already been sowing mines across the shipping routes. On 5 August the crew of *Amphion* and her flotilla sighted the enemy vessel and, in firing what were probably the first shots of the war, sank it. In the process they rescued over forty German sailors who would become the first prisoners of war. As they were brought on board they looked so miserable that the captain took pity on them and issued each of them a ration of rum. Ironically, as the vessel was returning to Harwich on the following day, she struck some of the mines that had been laid by *Königin Louise*, and sank with the loss of about 150 men and about twenty of the German crew that had been rescued.

The bill that confirmed the order for amalgamation of the three towns received royal assent on 10 August. Mr Balfour-Browne, who had led the campaign to maintain Devonport's independence and resisted amalgamation, called for the House of Lords committee to reject the measure. Referring to Mr Ellis, the Town Clerk, he said that he thought England was a free country, 'until I made the acquaintance of the Kaiser of Plymouth.' The attitude of the latter authority, he remarked, was similar to that of a great European power negotiating on similar principles at the present time with small countries such as Belgium. He had to concede defeat but, while he obviously spoke with tongue in cheek, others might have wondered whether his light-hearted comments likening the Town Clerk to the man who would shortly be held responsible for the outbreak of war and thus the deaths of thousands were altogether in good taste at such a sensitive time.

On 30 August the first Red Cross hospital train arrived at Friary Station, full of wounded British and German soldiers from the front. Crowds had gathered to see it pull in as a fleet of buses, cars and ambulances waited to take them to temporary hospital accommodation at Salisbury Road School. Hyde Park Road School was likewise made a temporary hospital for the duration of the war, while Prince Rock and other schools were turned into temporary barracks. Cases of distress among women and children came to the attention of the welfare authorities, and it was found that their men had gone away to fight without having made reasonable provision for them first. Wives of leading service personnel wasted no time in setting up voluntary organisations to help them.

Among those who were particularly active in the provision of hospital work throughout Plymouth, and arranging shelter and accommodation for

Wounded soldiers arriving at Friary Road Station and being taken by stretcher to an ambulance, autumn 1914.

wounded servicemen, were Viscount and Viscountess Astor. The former, who had been Unionist Member of Parliament for Plymouth Sutton since 1910, applied no less than five times to enlist in the army, but was rejected because of a weak heart. As local MP, he could console himself with the thought that knowledge of his constituency and local people meant that he was able to provide a far more valuable service to the war effort at home than as just one of many military personnel on the Western Front.

Civilians would soon feel the impact of the fighting on their day-to-day lives. The Aliens Restriction Act required enemy nationals of military age to be interned, and others to be repatriated. Other aliens were forbidden to travel more than 5 miles from their place of residence, and required to register at their local police station.

Four days after the declaration of war, the Defence of the Realm Act (DORA) was swiftly passed by parliament, in effect suspending all existing constitutional safeguards for civil rights and liberties which were enjoyed as a matter of course in peacetime. People could be charged with breaking security regulations if caught or suspected of such normally innocent activities as flying a kite, buying binoculars, lighting a bonfire, discussing naval and military matters in public, or 'by word of mouth or in writing spreading reports likely to cause disaffection or alarm among any of His Majesty's forces or among the civilian population', and even feeding wild animals with bread, on the grounds that it would be wasteful. The police had the power to stop and question civilians if they suspected any infringement of regulations, and those who refused to cooperate could be detained and even imprisoned. Strict censorship was imposed by the Admiralty and the War Office, with major restrictions on what war news the press was permitted to publish.

Alcoholic beverages were watered down, and restrictions were imposed on pub opening times which would remain in force until a new Licensing Act seventy-six years later. The Plymouth Watch Committee kept a close eye on any Sunday trading in the town. Anyone found selling goods on the Sabbath was liable to be reported to the police, and the shopkeeper would generally be prosecuted. The military authorities became concerned when people were getting drunk and were suspicious that someone might be plying them with drinks in order to extract information. Major Penton issued an order that civilians were forbidden to offer drink to the men, and it would be an act of mistaken kindness to do anything which prevented members of the armed forces from performing their duty to the Empire. Any publicans who served liquor to a man that was likely to render him unfit for fighting would be 'severely dealt with', and the Licensed Victuallers' Association asked soldiers to refrain from standing their comrades drinks, as they would have done in peacetime.

Wounded soldiers being unloaded by stretcher from an ambulance, a converted London bus, outside Salisbury Road Hospital, autumn 1914.

Barbed wire entanglements and stacks of sandbags were placed around the town boundaries, while trenches were dug along the coast. As in the Napoleonic Wars a century earlier, there were fears of invasion, with the possibility of Plymouth and other coastal towns being bombarded from the sea. To defend against the possibility of enemy attack, the military presence was increased in these areas. Additional troops were stationed at Fort Bovisand, with guns and searchlights at Jennycliff to protect the eastern entrance to Plymouth Sound. Sentries were armed and patrolled along the defence establishments such as the offices at Mount Wise Parade, where the Royal Navy offices were situated. If anybody approached a sentry he or she would be challenged, and if they could not provide a good reason for being there or were thought to be acting suspiciously, they risked arrest. Orders were given that the lights on Plymouth Hoe had to be extinguished every night by 10.00 p.m.

At Plymouth Fortress, the commanding officer issued an order demanding that all owners of motor vehicles in the town were required to offer their transport immediately to the Army Service Corps, or else their vehicles would be forcibly taken from them. These vehicles were used by the troops and the Western Home Defences, and would sometimes be seen laden with stores as they travelled in convoy through the main streets of the town. Some car owners, unaware of the military power of compulsory purchase, questioned the order. Despite the resultant shortage of personal transportation parents still encouraged their children to continue to attend school using alternative means of transportation where necessary. However, many children suddenly found they had unexpectedly longer school holidays, while the education authorities were frustrated by a shortage of caretakers and teachers, many of whom had joined up to go and fight.

By the end of August there were fears that aerial warfare would be conducted over Britain by the Germans, using aeroplanes and airships flying from bases on the coasts of Belgium and France. With her proximity to Devonport Dockyard, Plymouth was always considered a potential target for aerial attack from an enemy force operating from bases in north-west Europe. As bad news from the war intensified, so did unfounded rumours, such as that there was likely to be an imminent shortage of tea, or that all water for domestic use had been poisoned by the enemy.

In September Plymouth suffered another disaster at sea. On 22 September three armoured cruisers, which had been involved in action off Heligoland, were on patrol duty off the Dutch coast when they were sighted by a German submarine. One of them, HMS *Aboukir*, was struck by a torpedo and sank. A Devonport ship, HMS *Hogue*, was one of two which arrived and lowered its boats to rescue survivors, when it was hit by another torpedo and sank within three minutes. The third British cruiser was also hit, and the total death toll of sailors from this incident alone was almost 1,500.

The arrival of the Canadian Expeditionary Force on 14 October 1914 caused great interest in the town. All service-related comings and goings were keenly watched, and never before had such a large concentration of shipping entered Plymouth Sound. Comprising a convoy consisting of thirty-three liners with at least 25,000 men (some estimates suggest nearer 30,000) on board, it had crossed the Atlantic Ocean in eleven days and originally planned to dock at Southampton. Because of German submarine activity in the Channel, with U-boat sightings off Cherbourg and the Isle of Wight, it was diverted to Plymouth and steamed into the Sound and then into the dockyard to let the men disembark. Until the two lead ships, which had steamed ahead of the main convoy, passed the Breakwater at about 8.00 a.m., nobody outside the naval and military command knew what was happening. First to come was an Atlantic liner packed with troops, followed by a small ship carrying horses and stores. By midday, the remaining vessels formed an unbroken line stretching from Penlee Point to the Eddystone lighthouse. Several tugs had been assembled off Penlee Point to tow the troopships up the Hamoaze to moorings which were usually occupied by warships. Workers in the dockyard downed tools and went to the sea walls to cheer them on their way.

A leader in *The Times* remarked that the arrival of the Canadians in Plymouth was:

> The first answer given in Europe to Germany's egregious delusion that the Dominions would not rally to England in this war ... Canada does not stand alone in her conviction that this war is hers as well as ours, and that she is fighting for her own rights and liberties as truly as ourselves.

Many people carried the memory of the morning for a long time to come. Some twenty years later Marjorie Taylor, who had been aged 13 at the time, recalled that the slopes of the Hoe and the foreshore were a mass of cheering civilians, who stayed there throughout what was a warm sunny day. 'Hardly had the cheering started from shore than it was answered from the ships. The [Canadian] Highlanders on board played popular airs on the bagpipes, and the Sound was a medley of cheering and music.'

Once they had arrived on land, some of the Canadians left for Salisbury Plain, while others stayed in Plymouth for a few days. Among those who had just arrived were a few recent emigrants who were glad to have this opportunity of seeing family and friends in the town again, even if it was only for a short time. Plymothians were immediately struck by their informal manner, and 'the spirit of camaraderie between officers and men was most notable'. It seemed very different from the class-conscious British Army, in which the officers were so keen to preserve a demarcation line between themselves and the infantry.

On the morning of Sunday, 18 October, a battalion of 1,200 men from the Edmonton contingent marched from the dockyard, through Devonport and Union Street, with their band in front, to the Hoe for a church parade. The formed a square with the band playing in the centre, surrounded by several thousand civilians who joined them in singing hymns including 'Onward, Christian Soldiers' and 'Eternal Father, Strong to Save'. This was followed by an address in which the colonel said the Canadians had come to help the English who had always stood by them, in the fight she had nobly undertaken 'in the cause of liberty and small nations', and that the war in which they were engaged was 'a righteous one for God and Liberty'. Sadly, many of these men would be killed six months later in the first gas attack of the war at the Battle of Ypres.

The naval losses of August and September were only a foretaste of what was to come. Several families lost loved ones in the next major disasters. HMS *Monmouth*, another Devonport-manned ship, and HMS *Cape of Good Hope*, were both lost in the Battle of Coronel off the coast of Chile, fought on 1 November. Both ships went down with no survivors.

Christmas decorations at Salisbury Road Hospital, 1914.

It was the first significant defeat to be suffered by the British Royal Navy for over a century. A few days later the dreadnought cruisers HMS *Invincible* and HMS *Inflexible* sailed from Scapa Flow to Devonport where they were fitted out, in record time, to take part in the Battle of the Falkland Islands on 8 December. This helped to redress the balance when the British fleet achieved a notable victory at sea.

Although much of the war news so far had been sombre, that Christmas there was no lack of presents and fancy goods in the shops in Plymouth. Even though prices had risen sharply, there was no significant food shortage. Yet many families had to celebrate with loved ones far away, serving at the front or at sea. A mood of optimism still existed among some that the war would soon be over and they would be reunited before long. Few could have imagined that peace was almost four long and bitter years ahead.

On 25 November 1914 Devonport was delighted to welcome the arrival of *Jason*, a United States collier, or a 'Santa Claus ship'. Escorted by a flotilla of destroyers, she came bearing a cargo of about 5 million toys and Christmas gifts for the children of the belligerent European powers. The dolls, games, and articles of clothing had been collected by people all over America to send to those on the other side of the Atlantic, including those in Germany and Austria as well as Britain, France, Belgium and Russia. It was largely as a result of the initiative of William O'Loughlin of the *Chicago Herald*, who was travelling onboard ship as a special commissioner in charge. After the ship anchored at the naval barracks to offload those gifts intended for children in Britain, she was due to proceed to Marseilles and after that to Genoa, from where the remaining cargo could be distributed. The officers and Mr O'Loughlin were entertained to dinner that evening at the Royal Hotel.

Among those fighting in the trenches in Europe were men from the 1st and 2nd Battalions of the Devonshire Regiment, and doubtless men from Plymouth among them, who took part in the Christmas truce on the Western Front. British and German soldiers called out festive greetings to each other, sang carols, and exchanged food, tobacco, alcohol, and souvenirs such as hats and buttons, while a few even played spontaneous games of football. These truces generally lasted for only twenty-four hours from Christmas Eve, but in a few instances continued until New Year's Day before hostilities broke out again.

Ever since the start of hostilities, there was an ever-present need for new ships to be built at Devonport Dockyard. The most famous of these was the 27,500-ton battleship HMS *Royal Oak*, launched in November 1914 and commissioned on 1 May 1916 to form one of the Fourth Battle Squadron at the Battle of Jutland. This vessel survived the First World War and lasted until the opening skirmishes of the Second. At the dockyard the cruiser *Cleopatra* was also built at this time, as were two K-class submarines, which were both designed to steam at the same speed as the battle fleet. On trials in the basin at Keyham one of these, K-6, submerged and remained on the bottom for two hours. Although the faults were quickly repaired by an inspector of engine fitters aboard, the yard men refused to dive in her again.

Ocean liners continued to arrive in Plymouth, although the number of vessels calling was considerably less than it had been in peacetime. Weapons and supplies regularly arrived at Devonport to be loaded on to ships, among them Short 184 seaplanes destined for the Dardanelles. Although Plymouth was a prohibited area for aliens, the occasional foreign subject still entered the town. At a lodging house on the Barbican, the owner was prosecuted for failing to register the name and nationality of a person who was considered an alien. German spies were said to be entering England disguised as Belgian refugees and, in October 1914, Plymouth Corporation was officially notified by the Home Office that as a result they were not permitted to offer hospitality to people who claimed to be refugees from that country.

2nd Battalion of the Devonshire Regiment in 1912, soldiers of No.4 Section, 'F' Company at Stonehouse Barracks.

The dispensary at General Military Hospital, Salisbury Road.

On 8 September 1914 King George V and Queen Mary paid a visit to Devonport, arriving in the royal train on a two-day visit. The first royal family engagement in the country since the outbreak of war, it began with an inspection of troops and the presentation of decorations at the Brickfields, followed by a tour of seven military and naval hospitals visiting sick and wounded servicemen. At the end of the first day the king and queen departed in the royal train from Devonport to Horrabridge, but came back to Plymouth North Road Station next day to visit more hospitals in the morning, and watch a parade and march past at Devonport in the afternoon. After the ceremony the king presented nine men with the Distinguished Service Medal, then proceeded through the dockyard to see the ships and visit workshops.

3

ESPIONAGE AND PETTY CRIME

It was inevitable that some civilians, as well as persons of foreign birth, would fall foul of the wartime restrictions in various ways. One of the most remarkable cases in Plymouth was that of a lady known as Princess von Wrede, staying at the Grand Hotel on the Hoe, who was suspected of being a German spy. Her presence came to the attention of Lieutenant Colonel W.F. Drury, a Royal Marines officer attached to the intelligence department at Devonport whose duties included the investigation of any reports about suspect aliens in their midst. A woman whose husband worked at the passport office asked what he had done with 'the Austrian Princess', as she told him her husband had recently refused to issue a passport to a Princess von Wrede on the grounds of her undesirability.

Although she had been in Plymouth for several weeks, the local police had failed to notify the intelligence department of her presence, as she had not registered with them in accordance with the practice that 'aliens' needed to make themselves known to the authorities. Drury went to check the Grand Hotel register, and confirmed that she was indeed staying there, registered as 'de Wrede'. Next day Drury, along with two senior Scotland Yard officers attached to Devonport Intelligence, entered the Grand Hotel and arrested her on a charge of having contravened the Defence of the Realm Act. On further investigation it appeared that she had been given French naturalisation papers in error by the French government. While she was being interviewed at the police station, two police officers made a thorough search of her hotel room. While doing so they found several thousand pounds' worth of jewellery and a number of letters.

When she appeared in court, it emerged that she was Austrian-born, had been married first to a Polish citizen, then had the union annulled and took

Prince von Wrede as her second husband. Her Polish ex-husband brought the case to the Court of Appeal in Paris, where the original marriage was upheld, with the result that she was not really a princess after all. She was still, therefore, legally the wife of a Polish national and, as neither of them had ever been French nationals, the French police admitted that their government had made an error, although rather oddly she continued to be represented in court by the French consul.

Most of the letters discovered in her room were quite innocent, but they included one torn note which she had probably meant to destroy and somehow omitted to do so. Written in German, it was from an officer in the Prussian army, thanking her for having provided him with hospitality at her villa in northern France during the recent German advance, and saying how pleasant it had been to come across a German house in France. During the hearing, Drury produced this in court. As it was read out, the accused and her solicitors protested. The Chairman of the Court tried to rule Drury's evidence as irrelevant and refused to let a French detective give supporting evidence, but Drury insisted that he must be allowed to continue. He proceeded to give evidence that the daughter of the accused was the wife of the chief of staff of Moritz von Bissing, the German governor of Belgium, while her mother remained at liberty in Plymouth, having secured permission from the Foreign Office to communicate directly with the wife of a senior enemy army officer.

Astonishingly, she was merely fined £5. On hearing the verdict, she exclaimed contemptuously, 'Five pounds, there is twenty for your poor box.' Even more surprisingly in view of the evidence presented against her, the Chief Constable of Plymouth raised no objection to her remaining in the area, and she was allowed to return to the Grand Hotel. She stayed there for a short time, before leaving for London. Fearing that she still had the potential to cause further mischief, Drury contacted Scotland Yard, but she could not be traced. Five years later, he was told by the French secret police that she had been arrested again in France, though on what charge was never made clear.

Other refractions were dealt with more swiftly. That same year, Private Richard Bentley was stopped by police at Millbay Station as he was buying a train ticket for his home town of Derby. When questioned he admitted that he was a deserter, and had previously been placed under detention for fourteen days. After appearing before the Justices at Plymouth he was handed over to the military authorities for further punishment. Those who asked whether there was one law for the rich and another for the poor would certainly have had good reason for so doing.

At Christmas 1915 a mood of gloom settled over the city, made worse by heavy rain. It was observed that there were fewer people out on the streets carol singing than in previous years. Nevertheless butchers and poulterers with large stocks quickly sold out, although meat was fetching higher prices than it had in the previous year.

There would be no relaxation in the treatment of those who did not adhere strictly to security regulations. In January 1916 Dorothy Bowles, of Plympton, was stopped and charged with having used headlights on her car in Tavistock Road within 6 miles of the coast, in contravention of an order under the Defence of the Realm Act. (People were also liable to prosecution if caught sketching within a similar distance of the sea.) When she appeared in court, she said she had understood from regulations obtained from London that she was permitted to use headlights if tissue paper was placed on the inside of the glass, as she had done. She had been driving with her sidelights on until she reached North Road, only switching the headlights on after she had narrowly avoided running over two pedestrians in the darkness. Despite these mitigating circumstances, she was fined £1.

Six months later two women who lived in Stonehouse were summoned in separate cases for failing to screen the lighting in their rooms. A police constable reported that their lights had been visible half a mile away after 11.30 p.m. one night. Leah Penfold said that her husband had recently joined up, she had not been home very long that evening, and the baby had just fallen out of bed. Sarah Coe apologised, explaining that she and her husband had forgotten about the blinds that night. The chairman of the magistrates reminded the police that both women and their families were living in small houses, and that the occupants of larger dwellings were also infringing regulations on a much greater scale. Both were discharged with a caution.

Further petty crimes were reported with transgressors similarly being brought before the courts. In January 1918 Bessie Mackintosh and Frances Bond, both of Martin Street, were charged by the magistrates with loitering in George Street and persistently importuning. They pleaded not guilty, but a policeman said that they had been observed stopping several American sailors. Another constable told the court that they had been cautioned for the same offence on several previous occasions and had also been taken to the Salvation Army Home. One of the women was infected with venereal disease, and because of her record would be deported from Plymouth, a fate which had befallen twenty-nine other women charged with or suspected of prostitution in the previous nine months. Among other wartime restrictions, in the interests of the health of servicemen, attempts were made to re-enact the Contagious Diseases Act, abolished in 1886, which meant that women believed to be prostitutes could be made to undergo compulsory medical examinations for venereal disease.

Another restriction during wartime, or as some might have seen it a restriction of individual liberty, was that relating to the ownership of animals. Anybody who owned a horse, whether for riding or farming purposes, was liable to lose it as it would be requisitioned for war service, to be used as transport or in cavalry charges. Over 8 million taken in this way were killed during the four years of fighting, but over 2.5 million injured animals were successfully treated by vets. However, many people who were required to give up their beloved animals never saw them again.

Places of entertainment were not curtailed and remained little affected by the conflict, largely as it was considered vital to provide such facilities in order to keep up the morale of both servicemen and civilians at such a time. The Palace Theatre in Union Street, built in 1898 with a capacity of nearly 2,000, played to full or almost full houses throughout the war years, with Marie Lloyd, Lillie Langtry, Adelaide Hall, Rob Wilton and other music-hall stars regularly appearing on the stage. As there was a shortage of male acts during the war, some shows had to be produced as revues with a predominantly female cast.

4

THE CONFLICT INTENSIFIES

Early in the new year of 1916 there was increasing concern about the possibility of Zeppelins, or giant German airships, carrying out raids on Plymouth. During the previous year London and the east coast had been targeted, with considerable damage to property and some casualties. In response to public demands as to what measures were being taken to combat attacks if they should come, the government organised a chain of defences comprising searchlights and fighter stations linked to control centres. At Devonport the Commander-in-Chief proposed that a committee should be formed comprising the Garrison Commander, the Plymouth Town Clerk and representatives of the gas and electric light companies, to consider arrangements which would black out the town as well as neighbouring districts such as Saltash and Torpoint if necessary.

At various stages it was reported that Zeppelins were approaching south-west England, although on investigation most of these proved to be errors of identification. Though the town was never attacked, there was one false alarm that brought it to a halt. A naval plane which had not been notified to the military passed up the coast, and an order was sent out to take all defensive measures. During the evening rush hour, all traffic on the town roads and all trains then running came to a complete stop. Crowds were trapped in the streets and stations, unable to move for a couple of hours, until the mistake was discovered and an all-clear was given.

In February 1916 a night exercise was held over Plymouth to test defences in case of an attack. At midnight the alarm was sounded by a series of short blasts from whistles and sirens, with guns fired at ten-second intervals. The public were warned not to rush out into the streets, traffic would be required to stop when the lights went out, and horses were to be unharnessed from carriages and carts. Arrangements had been made to switch off the electric light at the power station, but not to extinguish gas lamps in the streets, which still burnt as brightly as ever.

At the end of that same month the Devonport authorities received a telegram from Dartmouth Coastguard to say that Zeppelins had been sighted heading west. However, it was later understood that it was a simple matter of a British airship which had failed to declare its identity.

Royal Marine detachments from Plymouth were active in various theatres of war, including the battles of the Falkland Islands and Jutland, and a Plymouth battalion formed part of a Royal Marines brigade serving in Belgium and France. Every family in Plymouth was affected by the mounting casualty lists. All the major sea battles involved Devonport ships and men to some extent, and soldiers from the 2nd Devon Regiment were fighting on the front line in France. While the threat of invasion was slight, the War Office still considered it important to put into operation a precautionary defence scheme. It was thought that the sea approaches to Plymouth were more or less impregnable. The eastern approach was closed by a boom and nets, and the western entrance was heavily guarded. At first a guard was placed on railway bridges and viaducts, and road blocks were set up on all main roads leading to Plymouth, as precautions against spies and saboteurs. However, the town suffered little inconvenience, the sea approaches were never disturbed, and ships passed in and out of the Sound unhindered.

The Battle of Jutland, fought in May 1916, resulted in a loss of fourteen ships to the Royal Navy, several of them Devonport-manned, as well as 6,274 men. One ship involved was the 26,000-ton battle cruiser *Lion*, flagship of Vice-Admiral Sir David Beatty. A Devonport-built vessel, manned by local men, it was badly damaged when one of its gun turrets was struck by a shell igniting cordite charges, but saved from destruction by the heroic actions of turret officer Major F. Harvey, who ordered a magazine to be flooded. He died of his wounds, and was awarded a posthumous Victoria Cross. Other Devonport-built ships involved in the action at Jutland included HMS *Defence*, destroyed by gunfire and with her entire crew of some 900 killed, HMS *Warrior*, sunk with the loss of over a hundred, HMS *Nomad*, from which eighty-four of her crew were taken by the Germans as prisoners of war after she was sunk, HMS *Indefatigable*, sunk with a loss of about 1,000 men and very few survivors, HMS *Minotaur*, HMS *Temeraire*, HMS *Collingwood*, HMS *Centurion*, and HMS *Marlborough*. In the German fleet, the *Ancona* and the *Frauenlob*, two light cruisers which had taken part in the naval visit of 1904, were both sunk.

Around this time the Admiralty decided to look for possible sites in or near Plymouth which might be suitable for mooring airships. The most suitable was thought to be the racecourse at Chelson Meadow, next to Saltram Park estate, with the minor disadvantage that it was some distance from the Royal Naval Barracks at Devonport, where the airship landing party would be accommodated. Others which were considered were the Brickfields, Devonport, owned by the War Department and near to the barracks but also too close to electric tram lines; an area at Ernesettle, but inappropriate as it was prone to dangerous air currents; and finally a field at Admiralty Lane, Trevol, near Torpoint. The Chelson site was considered the most suitable, and an airship sub-station was established there, with a balloon base at Merrifield, Torpoint, where balloon sheds and store rooms were erected. Personnel from the RNAS were accommodated in the hulk of HMS *Valiant* anchored in the Tamar. The balloons were used for observation purposes and flown from cables up to a distance of about a mile high. The balloonatists, as they were known, stood in a basket suspended beneath the balloon, and the observer on a canvas slung seat.

Airships were moored to the trees. Around twenty airmen served at the station, accommodated in the racecourse stand, where they slept on hard benches. The airships were regularly seen over South Devon, out on their patrols.

An airship above Chelson Meadow, *c.* 1917.

Two Sea Scout (SS) non-rigid ships were moored at Laira, specially built to search for submarines in coastal waters, providing air cover that the RNAS aircraft could not because of their limits of endurance. The SS Class airships could fly for eight hours with a small bomb load at a maximum speed of 50mph. A crew of two sat in the suspended car, with the telegraph operator in the front seat and the pilot in the rear.

In April 1917 each air station in the South Western Group was made a separate command, with headquarters at Devonport, under the Commander-in-Chief. Routine patrols by airships, seaplanes and aeroplanes were introduced to cover the vulnerable areas. Special seaplane patrols, working in cooperation with destroyers and motor launches, were also organised. At about the same time the Admiralty decided to open seaplane stations and airfields in the south-west of England. It had only been six years since the first seaplane, an Avro D piloted by a Royal Navy commander, was successfully flown in England, and in 1912 the Royal Navy only had three hydroplanes.

In June 1917 the Americans took over Victoria Wharf as a base and operated a large number of mass-produced submarine chasers. Within weeks two destroyers and over sixty submarine chasers were based there, with over 3,000 men working from the port and headquarters in Elliot Terrace. Many Q-ships, decoy vessels or armed merchant ships whose purpose was to lure submarines into surface attacks and then sink them, operated from Devonport, though their activities were kept a closely-guarded secret.

Early in the war a Royal Naval Air Service base, RNAS Laira, had been established at Chelson Meadow, a sub-station of the base at Mullion on the Lizard Peninsula, Cornwall. The base was home to two airships, which were moored to the trees and painted in a camouflage khaki, brown and black. Meanwhile, at the Cattewater a seaplane base had been established in September 1913, a little earlier, and several trial flights were made from there. The area available at Chelson soon proved inadequate, and a larger area was required for the necessary facilities. The south-west coast was regarded as particularly vulnerable to German submarines and, as the other naval air stations were located on the east and south-east coasts, it was clear that another was needed. The peninsula at Mount Batten was considered the most suitable as regards location, especially as Plymouth Sound would provide a suitable take-off and alighting area. Towards the end of 1916 the land was requisitioned from its owner, much to the disappointment of the public who had long enjoyed the beach facilities. RNAS Cattewater, comprising four seaplane hangars, as well as workshops and slipways for the planes, was established in February 1917. It was under the control of a large RNAS establishment at Tregantle, Cornwall. The officers were billeted in a row of coastguard cottages overlooking Plymouth Sound, while Castle Inn, facing the Cattewater, became the residence of the Station Commander.

On 1 April 1918 the RNAS merged with the Royal Flying Corps to become the Royal Air Force. RAF Cattewater came into existence, the unit at Tregantle in Cornwall was closed, and headquarters were transferred to Mount Wise Barracks.

That same month Earl Fortescue, Lord Lieutenant of Devon, accompanied by the Mayor of Plymouth, and a large gathering of civic and service representatives, assembled for a ceremony on Plymouth Hoe at which a number of decorations would be presented to men in the town. Among the recipients were five dockyard workers, who were awarded the British Empire Medal for the work on submarine trials. Another received the BEM for dealing promptly with an explosion that occurred on diving operations, also during submarine trials. Two others received awards for bravery in refloating a damaged ship that had run aground during a storm, while another was given the BEM for prompt action in dealing with an explosion in a Plymouth munitions factory where 140 men were working and could easily have been killed.

As the war in France continued, so did the casualties among British soldiers. At the Battle of the Bois des Buttes in May 1918, the 2nd Devon Regiment lost many men as well as their commander, Colonel Anderson-Morshead, the scion of an old Plymouth merchant family. The names of the military personnel who had been killed in action would be remembered on the war memorial which was later erected on the Hoe.

Yet there was some consolation to be taken from the fact that, by the summer, some of the senior military commanders perceived that the central powers were close to conceding defeat.

5

THE END OF
THE WAR

Nonetheless, another enemy was about to claim human lives on a massive scale. By summer 1918, most countries in the war-weary continent were beginning to suffer from the ravages of a severe influenza epidemic. There were indications that an epidemic had started in England and, by the end of July, thirty-five deaths had been reported in Plymouth. Nevertheless, most cases reported during the summer were comparatively mild, and many of those infected would recover within about three days of showing the symptoms.

During the autumn a lethal strain of the virus, known as Spanish influenza, appeared. Some patients became ill, then briefly made good progress before suffering a relapse within twenty-four hours, with death occurring a little later due to acute pulmonary infection. Others, who had generally enjoyed good health, might wake in the morning feeling slightly unwell, go to work or about their normal business during the day, and be dead by the evening. In October and November alone 432 influenza-related deaths were reported in Plymouth. On 20 October 1918 R.A.J. Walling, editor of the *Western Daily Mercury*, wrote to his son Captain R.V. Walling, that 'There's a fearful epidemic of flu in Plymouth and half the office is out of commission'. Born in Plymouth, the latter had followed his father into journalism, becoming a junior reporter on the paper before joining the army and serving on the Western Front, where he was a captain in the territorial branch of the Royal Garrison Artillery and wounded at the Battle of Passchendaele the previous year.

By this time Germany and the central powers were beginning to admit that this was a conflict they could not win, and it was apparent that all would soon be over. Newspaper headlines made it increasingly evident that there were grounds for optimism that the long-awaited tidings would soon be with them. After a few false alarms, shortly after 9.00 a.m. on 11 November the massed sound from ships' sirens and whistles, joined by factories and warships in harbour, signalled to everyone that the conflict was over at last. One 9-year-old schoolboy, walking briskly along College Road in Mutley that morning, was anxious he would be late for class until he heard the sirens, arrived at school and found most of the pupils being sent home. A teacher patted him on the back and told him that there would be no lessons that day.

Although no proclamation had yet been made anywhere in the town, flags were already being hung from windows of private houses everywhere as well as from the main buildings and business premises in the centre, and strings of bunting were hung across the roads in celebration. Shops did a brisk trade in Union Jacks and in the flags of the Allied powers, as members of the public came in to buy whatever was available, placed their money on the counter, and went out without bothering to collect their change. Several businesses were unable to keep pace with the demand. Church and school bells rang out at intervals, and continued to do so for the rest of the day. Crowds in their thousands congregated in New George Street outside the offices of the *Western Morning News* to wait for an official announcement to be published. At 11.00 a.m. news arrived from the Admiralty at Mount Wise, where senior personnel telephoned the newspaper staff which then placed a notice in the window of their offices.

Crowds were gathering in Guildhall Square, made up equally of servicemen, civilians and schoolchildren who were delighted to have the day off and realised that here was history in the making. Contingents of Boy Scouts and Girl Guides were wheeled into the square by their superiors, and formed a rallying point for others. According to a *Western Morning News* reporter, 'Khaki and hospital blue intermixed with the navy blue of seamen, gay dresses of ladies, and the waving of innumerable flags by children, flanked by the time-worn walls of St Andrew's church tower and the Guildhall in the background.' At 11.30, surrounded by aldermen, councillors, and men from the town clerk's office, the Mayor of Plymouth, Alderman J.P. Brown, confirmed that an armistice had been signed at 5.00 a.m., and hostilities had ceased from 11.00 a.m.. With this, the fighting and bloodshed were over. He called for cheers for the king, for Marshal Foch, Supreme Commander of the Allied Armies, and the Allied navies and armies.

Most of the shops were deserted for a while and business seemed at a standstill. By the afternoon many offices had closed for the day, as those staff who were still attempting to work could not concentrate because of the cheerful sounds ringing throughout the streets outside, and employers found

Devonport Dockyard, decorated with bunting at the end of the war in November 1918.

Australian troops, waiting at Millbay Docks to leave on the hospital ship *Soudan* at the end of the war.

that any efforts to carry on as usual were up against 'an irresistible force'. At Cattewater, all vessels in port likewise sported bunting, while one large vessel was firing rockets, and another did its best with a miniature gun.

As the scenes of rejoicing were taking place, two lorries carrying German prisoners of war were driving through the town centre and had to halt because of the crowds. Some thought the prisoners were totally devoid of expression either of sorrow or of joy, while others considered that they looked as pleased and relieved as anybody else as they guessed what was happening. Everyone standing around was magnanimous in showing due restraint towards the men who had until so recently been their foes.

A couple of Devonport servicemen, 1917. (Derek Tait)

Air Station Batten, Mount Batten.

After the Treaty of Versailles was signed on 28 June 1919, the fifth anniversary of the double assassination at Sarajevo which had helped to precipitate the years of conflict, 6 July 1919 was proclaimed Peace Sunday throughout Britain. Church services in Plymouth were packed. At St Andrew's church, the mayor and representatives of the municipality were present, while the Bishop of Exeter preached at an open air service in Guildhall Square, and the Royal Sailors' Rest, Devonport, was attended by the Commander-in-Chief and senior naval officers in port. On bank holiday Monday, 4 August, a Peace Carnival organised by the ratings and officers of the local naval camp was held at St Budeaux, with several people taking part in sports and others attending in fancy dress.

Although the war was over, local service establishments were maintained in accordance with the basic requirements of national defence. By April 1922 the one remaining squadron at RAF Mount Batten had been disbanded, and the base was turned over to a Care and Maintenance Unit. This was expected to be the end of the base, but after the Cattewater Seaplane Station Bill was enacted in 1923 it reopened on 1 October 1928 as RAF Mount Batten. In April 1935 it became the Fleet Air Arm's floatplane base, with a total strength of twenty-three officers and 203 airmen. In October 1938 work began on constructing underground oil tanks at Radford Quarry for the use of RAF Mount Batten, and in January 1940 a pipeline was opened from Turnchapel Wharf to the tanks.

By this time, the people of Plymouth as well as of Great Britain had learnt to their cost that four years of fighting in the second decade of the century had not, after all, been 'the war to end wars'.

THE SECOND
WORLD WAR

1

THE APPROACHING MENACE

With the rise of Fascism throughout Europe during the 1930s, and growing alarm at events in Nazi Germany, an ever increasing air of unease hung over the country. While some were ready to dismiss talk of another war as mere alarmism, others were prepared for the worst. Political extremism was not confined to the European mainland, and the German and Italian dictators Hitler and Mussolini had their supporters throughout Britain. In the summer of 1933 a group of British Fascists held meetings on the pavement outside the main post office at Plymouth (which had been created a city in 1928). That November a Fascist headquarters office was opened in Lockyer Street, where the flowerbeds in the back garden were cleared and replaced with concrete so that the local contingent of Blackshirts could practise their drill. After increasingly rowdy and violent gatherings in Plymouth in 1934 the organisation's support rapidly dwindled, especially after the *Western Morning News*, angry at the rough handling one of its reporters received while trying to cover one such meeting, announced that it would no longer give the movement any publicity whatsoever. The Lockyer Street headquarters closed down soon afterwards.

Meanwhile, preparations for a worst-case scenario continued apace. There was a taste of the shape of things to come in the autumn of 1935 when a blackout exercise took place in Plymouth, and aircraft flew over the city to check its effectiveness in the event of an air raid. Three and a half years later, in April 1939, thirteen Great Western Railway trucks pulled into the goods station at Sutton Harbour, loaded with 9 tons of steel air-raid shelters. Six men were required to carry the parts for each, including straight and curved lengths of various sizes, T-shaped pieces, angles, and bags of nuts and bolts, and each household was responsible for constructing its own shelter.

Later that month parliament passed a Military Training Act which introduced conscription, with all men aged 20 and 21 required to undertake six months of military training.

Reporters who interviewed members of the public in Plymouth at around this time were surprised by the divergence of opinion they discovered. Some people, taking reassurance in the fact that no enemy power had invaded the country for nearly a thousand years, were sure it could never happen, and they dismissed air-raid precautions as a shocking waste of public money, especially at a time of such financial hardship. Others were convinced that it was better to be prepared.

By summer 1939 the area was on the alert to an increasingly precarious situation. The Air Raid Precautions organisation was set up, with responsibility for issuing gas masks, the upkeep of local public shelters, and the maintenance of the blackout. Ambulance attendants for ARP would also help to rescue people after air raids, administer first aid to casualties, search for survivors, and help to recover dead bodies. On the instructions of the Home Office, ARP workers who were engaged for eight hours per day and thus forty-eight hours per week were to be paid £3 weekly if they were men, and £2 for women. With nearly 1,500 people employed full-time in

A gas mask rescue drill. The mask was a vital accessory carried by everyone at all times in case of an enemy gas attack. (Derek Tait)

this capacity, by September the total weekly wages bill amounted to about £4,000 per week, with one-third of the cost borne by the city and two-thirds by the government.

Of all the holidaymakers who were making the most of the sunshine that season, few were aware that twenty-one warships of the Home Fleet had left Devonport and were sailing to their action stations, or that several thousand men in the Fleet Reserve had been called to Plymouth to man the warships. However, rumours of naval and military action were gradually spreading. By the end of August, people in Plymouth were shopping in their thousands for blackout material and local retailers could not keep pace with the demand. Blue bulbs were installed in Corporation buses in order to reduce the glow from lighted interiors during the blackout. Panic buying of food also set in, with stores in the city making several thousand deliveries to those who were prudently stocking up 'just in case'. Moreover, during the last weekend in August, the first of many deliveries of sand from Lee Moor was made at Plymouth. 1.6 million sandbags were being kept in order to protect public buildings, and 22,500 tons were due to be delivered altogether.

On 1 September, German troops invaded Poland, with whom Britain had signed a treaty of mutual assistance seven days earlier. That same day William Cornish, headmaster of Johnston Terrace School, Keyham, noted in the school's logbook that shortly after 4.00 p.m. he had received official notice that owing to hostilities between Germany and Poland, all schools would be closed until further notice. This would help officials to deal with allocating places to children who were being evacuated from London, as Plymouth and the West Country were thought to be a safe area to send children. In fact, schools would be able to reopen about three weeks later.

2

THE OUTBREAK OF WAR

On Sunday, 3 September 1939, the Prime Minister, Neville Chamberlain, broadcast from No. 10 Downing Street that Britain and Germany were now at war. That same day a congregation of eighty attended morning service at St Augustine's church, Lipson Vale. There would probably have been more present, but for the fact that some regular members were among the many who were sitting at home by their radios anxiously waiting to be told of what they had long feared. As Mr Clemmer, the sidesman, presented the collection plate, he whispered to the vicar that he had just heard the news. After a short silence they sang the hymn 'Breathe on me, Breath of God', while the worshippers knelt in prayer. The vicar then made a short statement, after which the National Anthem was sung. Later that day giant silver barrage balloons were hoisted up in the sky over Plymouth as a defence against enemy air attack. Soon they would be a familiar sight over the city and at other harbours in Devon where merchant ships, naval boats and amphibious invasion craft would be seen flying a balloon for protection. Anti-aircraft guns, searchlights and sound detectors, all part of the city's air defence, were kept at sites some distance away.

That same afternoon, a train carrying about 800 schoolchildren who were being evacuated arrived at North Road Station, to be greeted by a crowd including men and nurses from the St John Ambulance Brigade. Other passengers bought the youngsters sweets, chocolate and ice creams as they stopped for a break before continuing to the Camborne and Redruth areas in Cornwall. Also on the train were several mothers and small children, the youngest aged only 3 weeks.

On the day that war broke out, the city council placed advertisements for contractors to erect fifty brick or concrete posts for Air Raid Wardens.

Lady Astor with young evacuees at North Road Station. (Steve Johnson)

White's Naval Surplus Stores in Ebrington Street offered for sale a stock of 1,200 Government Surplus curtains, ready to hang, with prices from 6*d* to 10*d* each, or black-lined fancy linen, priced from 1*s* 6*d* to 3*s* 6*d*, and metal boxes which could be used for such purposes as storage for irreplaceable documents such as house deeds, or alternatively containers for food storage, at 1*s* or 2*s* depending on size.

An order was issued by the government which prevented people from gathering together in large crowds, and all cinemas were closed. This restriction was considered impossible to police, and the withdrawal of such an amenity was regarded as a severe blow to morale as well as to the thriving British film industry. Moreover, in the absence of television, as broadcasting had been closed down for the duration, the importance of films as a means of keeping the public informed of latest war news was readily appreciated.

For the second time in just over twenty-five years, the start of hostilities was viewed throughout the city with mixed feelings. All those old enough to remember the previous conflict were aware that any major military campaigns would mean the loss of able-bodied men leaving home to fight, many never to return. However, Plymouth itself had had the good fortune to remain otherwise relatively unscathed between 1914 and 1918, with no structural damage as a result of enemy action, and there was little reason to suppose that the situation would be different this time.

Additionally, for the unemployed it meant their long quest for work might be over. Once again, a full dockyard would require more labour for armament purposes, building and repairing warships, while for retailers there would doubtless be an influx of servicemen to bring spending money into the town. If the coming war was to follow a similar pattern to that of the First World War, some thought optimistically, such a state of affairs would probably be to Plymouth's advantage. Few if any had the most remote idea of just how devastating for the city the next few years would be.

As an early foretaste of local tragedies to come, the Devonport-manned aircraft carrier HMS *Courageous*, which was serving with the Home Fleet and deployed on anti-submarine patrol to the west of Ireland, was torpedoed by a German submarine and within minutes sank with the loss of 519 men, including many reservists and pensioners. Once the news was known, relatives anxiously scanned the list of survivors at the main gates of the Royal Naval Barracks at Devonport, while the less fortunate had to face the loss of husbands and fathers.

A few weeks later, the authorities in Plymouth began to rehearse methods of dealing with attack from the air. An Emergency Committee consisting of all three party leaders was set up and the Town Clerk, Colin Campbell, was appointed Air Raid Precautions Officer. Anti-aircraft batteries were established, barrage balloons were deployed, and air-raid sirens were put under single remote control at Greenbank police headquarters. One precaution, which had its light-hearted side but was still to be taken in earnest, was a warning on public notice boards that children were not permitted to imitate the warning signal of the air-raid siren.

Because of the call-up with able-bodied young men joining the services, the territorials and other units of national defence, shop staff throughout the city were depleted by an average of 25 per cent. By mid-September the requisitioning of nearly all lorries available to carry ARP materials and serve other official purposes made it increasingly difficult for major firms to deliver goods to their customers as they had in peacetime. Dingles restricted its deliveries, and other retailers purchased horses so they could serve their customers who lived outside the city. The city's Drapers' Association urged members of the public to try and purchase goods during daylight hours, as no attempt would be made to prolong opening hours after the blackout. Apart from those shops which generally closed for an hour at lunch, efforts were made to try and avoid additional midday closing, so as not to restrict shopping hours any more than necessary. Commodities were rising in price up to 10 per cent or even 15 per cent of pre-war prices, and at least one trader warned that the public would need to get used to such increases.

It would be all too easy for people to attribute it to blatant profiteering, but wholesalers and retailers had to compensate themselves for the high premiums they were required to pay during wartime.

There were so many planes and squadrons at RAF Mount Batten that the base became overcrowded and the Fleet Air Arm had to move back to Lee-on-Solent. By the outbreak of the Second World War there was a squadron of Sunderland flying boats stationed at Mount Batten, which patrolled the south-western approaches in partnership with the two squadrons at Pembroke Dock. On 9 September 1939 a Sunderland boat launched the first attack on a German U-boat in the Channel, and on 18 September another helped to rescue the crew off the SS *Kensington Court*, which had been torpedoed about 70 miles off the Isles of Scilly. The Sunderland's pilot, Flight-Lieutenant Barrett, dropped eight of his bombs on the spot where the U-boat had been submerged before he was able to land and pick up fourteen of the crew from the stricken cargo vessel. Every member of the crew was saved, and Barrett was awarded the Distinguished Flying Cross.

At the outbreak of war the lord mayor was G.S. Scoble, a Labour member of the city council. When he completed his term of office on 9 November 1939, the leaders of all three parties wanted as his successor someone who would personify unity at the head of local affairs. Their unanimous choice was Lord Astor, who had represented Plymouth Sutton as Unionist Member of Parliament from 1910 to 1919. On succeeding his father as Viscount Astor he had resigned his seat, resulting in a by-election won by his wife Nancy, the first woman elected to Westminster to take her seat. Although a lifelong Conservative he was on the progressive wing of the party, widely respected by members of all parties, and shared to a degree the Labour party's vision of comprehensive long-term planning in urban and rural areas. He agreed to serve in that capacity for the duration, and worked tirelessly within the city for the war effort.

Within a week of taking office, he realised it would be pointless to have many different appeals for local charities all competing with each other. Instead, he decided, there should be a single one, the Lord Mayor's Fund, administered by a representative committee which would receive and consider every application for worthy causes. To help raise money he proposed a covenant by which people would be encouraged to subscribe a certain sum each week or month, while groups of people in societies, offices, schools, factories, stores and workshops were asked to appoint officers to collect and forward their regular contributions. Before long the Fund was raising money at the rate of £10,000 per year.

On 18 December 1939 King George VI paid his first visit to Plymouth as sovereign. For security reasons there had been no general announcement in advance, and even correspondents from national newspapers who were officially accompanying him had been given no idea of their destination as they left London on Sunday night. Even naval ratings in Plymouth who would be most closely involved were not specifically told, and all that anybody knew was that certain guards of honour who would be required on duty next day had been 'told off', thereby enabling them to draw their own conclusions. It was strictly a low-key visit enabling the king to make a tour of the naval establishments. At Millbay Docks he spoke to several men and officers, then inspected the ranks at the Royal Naval Barracks, after which he was taken on brief tours of the Royal William Victualling Yard and the Royal Naval Engineering College at Manadon, before having dinner at Hamoaze House and leaving in the evening.

That Christmas, despite blackouts, war and price rises, retailers surpassed their hopes and expectations with regard to festive trade. Several contingents of servicemen who had been unexpectedly granted leave caused a welcome last-minute rush, with shops such as the department store Pophams and the drapers John Yeo & Co reporting particularly brisk business. Handkerchiefs and warm woollies were particularly in demand as presents from loved ones for their menfolk in the war, and an increase was noted in the sale of English-made goods, despite a sharp rise in prices.

On 30 January 1940 HMS *Ajax* sailed into Plymouth Sound under cover of darkness after seeing action against the pocket battleship *Graf Spee* in the Battle of the River Plate, Argentina. For security reasons, not until she was in Plymouth Sound was any announcement made to the public, and only a few journalists were made aware. However, word soon spread, and crowds flocked to come and give her a rapturous welcome. On 15 February HMS *Exeter*, which had been built in Devonport and was carrying a largely local crew, returned from the same theatre of war. She had also suffered serious damage in action, with the loss of sixty men, and needed to sail to the Falkland Islands for temporary repair before undertaking the long voyage across the Atlantic and home. She returned to a welcome from Winston Churchill, First Lord of the Admiralty, Sir Dudley Pound, First Sea Lord, and Sir John Simon, Chancellor of the Exchequer, who came on board before she docked. People rushed to the waterside to see, with every vantage point from Devonport Dockyard to Mount Batten being crowded, while brass bands also turned up to deliver a musical welcome.

The officers and men from both ships were given a civic reception in the Guildhall on 16 February. At the luncheon the commanding officer,

Captain Bell, spoke about what the crew had achieved, and paid tribute to their comrades who had been killed in action; 'I only wish that I had been able to bring them all back home, but some we left behind.' After a refit in Devonport, *Exeter* joined the First Cruiser Squadron in the Home Fleet, and later saw service in the Middle East. In March 1942 she was scuttled by the crew after action against overwhelming Japanese forces in the Dutch East Indies, during which fifty-four officers and men were lost.

When 204 Squadron left for North Africa it was replaced on 1 April 1940 by Number 10 Royal Australian Air Force Squadron, who stayed at Plymouth for the duration of the war, and did not leave the base until October 1945. By then its members had flown 4,553,860 nautical miles, undertaken 3,177 operational flights, and sunk five submarines. Before they left England they were awarded a crest by King George VI with the motto 'Strike First'.

On the resignation of Neville Chamberlain as Prime Minister, in May 1940, Winston Churchill succeeded him and Lord Astor was offered a post in the wartime government as Minister of Agriculture because of his commitment to the gradual nationalisation of agricultural land. He declined to accept on the grounds that his first duty was to the people of Plymouth.

During the summer a Plymouth Anti-Gossip and Will-to-Win campaign was launched. As there was now a large number of service people in the city, fears increased that gossip and careless talk from their relatives could lead to the revelation of vital movements by service units and other important secrets inadvertently leaking out. Meetings were called at the Guildhall and at various service establishments, at which the speakers would remind everyone how important it was not to tell anybody of troops and ship movements and other matters that might be common knowledge in service quarters.

By the time the Germans reached the English Channel in the summer of 1940, what had been known as the 'phoney war' was over. Only then did Plymouth seriously consider how vulnerable it was to enemy action.

On 2 June about 80,000 French troops, newly evacuated from Dunkirk, arrived at Turnchapel Station to await re-embarkation for France. The need to offer them appropriate hospitality placed some pressure on the city's resources, but such was the state of organisation that within a day or so of the men's arrival a canteen service was being provided in the docks, while people all over the city were ready to volunteer help by offering sleeping accommodation and baths. Just over two weeks later, at 5.30 p.m. on 18 June, the ex-Great Western Railway Channel Islands ferry *St Helier* anchored in Plymouth Sound, after diverting while on passage from Southampton to La Pallice on the French coast. When it sailed again later that evening to resume its mission, the captain was surprised to pass French ships of all types making haste for the English ports. The situation on land was deteriorating and shortly afterwards *St Helier* was attacked by two enemy planes. The crew replied with heavy fire from the ship's guns and scored hits on both planes, causing a bomb which had been intended for the ship to fall some way short. Aware that any attempt to embark troops would almost certainly end in disaster, the ship was ordered to sea, where it ran the gauntlet of an enemy submarine and a severe electrical storm. It finally arrived back in the relative safety of Plymouth Sound on 21 June.

From the end of May onwards large numbers of French civilian refugees were landing at the city, mostly Bretons who had fled from their homes as German forces advanced across north-west France. Many, aged only 17 or 18, had been urged to go by their parents, who had been taken prisoner by the Germans, and scrambled on board any seagoing craft that was available. It was reported that they said as one that France must never give up, and they intended to go on fighting on behalf of their country in England, which they were sure would ultimately win. They were offered food and temporary accommodation at the rest centres which had initially been prepared to care for those who would be left homeless by air raids, and were then sent to Liverpool until arrangements could be made to repatriate them to France once it was safe to do so.

Also arriving at Plymouth at the same time were Allied servicemen, mostly British, who had likewise been evacuated from north-west France under a rescue plan, codenamed Operation Cyclone. This also entailed a fleet of merchant ships and small craft assembling and sailing from Plymouth and Portsmouth to various ports in north-west France. A further convoy of ten ships sailed overnight from the north-west ports of France to Plymouth carrying 23,000 service personnel. An army officer on the hospital ship *St Andrew* was given a cabin and settled down on his cross-Channel journey, ready to dock at Millbay. When he reached Plymouth he saw the Sound was full of ships.

The city was now extremely crowded, and the service barracks were filled to capacity. Their numbers had also just been swelled by at least a hundred Polish men who had arrived from France to enlist in the exiled Polish navy, and were scheduled to move on to a camp at Westward Ho! Due to a last-minute change in orders, they had to stay in Plymouth and were hastily found accommodation instead at the United Services Orphanage which was being used at the time by the Canadians.

At the same time, several French warships were arriving in Plymouth. Among them was the battleship FS *Paris*, which had to be docked to repair a leak caused by a bomb which had exploded near the ship before it arrived at

Devonport. It was thought that she could be used in Atlantic naval operations, but an Admiralty survey revealed that she was in very poor condition and, as she would be of no value to the British, the Vichy government requested her return to France.

In addition to these there was a giant French submarine *Surcouf*. Launched in 1928, at the time she was the largest submarine in the world, armed with two 8-inch guns mounted in a power operated twin turret, crewed by 130 officers and men, with space for forty prisoners of war. France was, however, somewhat divided in its allegiance at the time. Some French sailors had no desire to fight in the war, and were keen to return home on their ships. General de Gaulle was rallying exiled Frenchmen and women to join the Free French Forces, but not everyone supported him, particularly as a Franco-German alliance was questioning the future of the French naval ships in Britain and certain North Atlantic ports. The French fleet at Oran, Morocco, was under the command of the pro-Vichy Admiral Darlan, who was thought to be a potential collaborator with Hitler and who might use the French navy to attack the British. Throughout England there was more than a little suspicion of the French, until it was certain that they among those who were solidly pro-British. This was exacerbated when Marshal Pétain, who would become leader of the Vichy regime which collaborated with the Nazis, said that within weeks Britain would be invaded and have its neck wrung like a chicken. Churchill dismissed this foolish prediction with the words, in a typically robust speech, 'Some chicken – some neck!'

Surcouf had originally sailed from Cherbourg to Dakar, then to Martinique, and to Jamaica, before going to Brest to have an engine replaced. While the vessel was in dock, members of the crew were advised that all was apparently lost on the battlefields of France. The commander said that he had received orders that they must either scuttle the ship, sink it in order to prevent it from being captured by the Germans, or else leave port. Those who were willing to leave were asked to hold up their hands. If nobody wanted to go, the ship would be sunk. Every hand was raised, and so the commander said that they would therefore join the English; they sailed to Devonport on 20 June. On arrival at Devonport they were met by a contingent of English sailors, who were highly suspicious of the motives and intentions of any vessel coming from France at such a delicate time, and were acting under instructions to take the vessel over. Tensions were riding high and the first British seaman to step aboard was shot dead by a French sailor, who was promptly clubbed to death with a rifle for his pains. Another French sailor had a hand placed over his mouth and was immediately handcuffed. The English sailors ordered them to surrender. When an officer came to see what was happening, he was shot dead.

On 4 July Winston Churchill announced that as the French warships at Oran on the Algerian coast had refused to surrender to the British fleet and were not prepared to scuttle their vessels, a force of British warships had shelled them, inflicting some damage and preventing the warships from being a viable fighting force. The attack meant that the French ships would not be in any condition to take part in the war if they came under enemy control. Around 1,500 French sailors were killed. On 3 July at Devonport, Royal Navy and Marine task forces boarded French naval vessels in Plymouth. The warships had been moved from anchorage in the Hamoaze to alongside jetties in the naval dockyard. When a British boarding party was sent to take over the *Surcouf*, shooting broke out, with three British sailors and one Frenchman killed as the British took command. The vessel remained at Devonport for a time, but later sailed across the Atlantic and was sunk in February 1942 while on a voyage from Bermuda.

3

THE FIRST
BOMBING RAIDS

Plymouth had long been recognised by the military as a key position in the south-west. A boom device was installed to prevent enemy amphibious craft from attempting to land directly in the city, and coastal batteries were sited to cover the approaches to Plymouth Sound. Gun batteries were divided into three fire commands, at Wembury, Drake and Rame. Any attack by the enemy in strength, landing at several places, would present a serious danger. It was thought probable that enemy landings would be made to the east and west of Plymouth, with the east side being more vulnerable, and enemy landings on beaches could easily be made in conjunction with German airborne troops dropped over Dartmoor. Stretches of open water on the rivers Tamar, Lynher and Plym caused concern as it was thought enemy troop-carrying flying boats could land there. An appeal was made to owners of small boats across the rivers to position their vessels as a barrier in order to prevent any enemy seaplanes from landing. Any fighting for the defence of Plymouth would be on foot as the military commander thought the terrain would be unsuitable for tank warfare.

On 30 June, the first siren alarm of the war sounded and the population made their way to the nearest shelter. It proved to be a false alarm. A second came on the morning of 4 July, the first to occur during the school day. The headmaster of Johnston Terrace School noted in the school's logbook that the children went to the shelter at 10.30 a.m. and stayed there for an hour, during which time they behaved very well.

Nevertheless, during the next four years sirens would sound at Plymouth over 400 times, and there would be fifty-nine bombing raids. The first of these came just before midday on 6 July 1940, when three bombs hit a block of eight houses on a housing estate at Swilly Road, Devonport, resulting in the destruction of three houses and severe damage to several nearby properties. Three people, a man, a woman and a boy were killed, and six others were injured. Nevertheless, children from London and the cities of the Midlands were being evacuated to Plymouth at this time, and as yet the authorities at Whitehall saw no need to send anyone out of the city. It was a source of bitterness for some time, even after the war, that while local councillors and organisations were pressing for children to be sent away from the area as part of a carefully organised evacuation scheme, the powers in London were slow to act and did not consider it a priority until enemy action was at its worst the following year.

On the afternoon of 7 July in a second raid, planes flew down the Plym Valley. One plane came so low that a man on duty at the gasworks at Coxside, which was evidently the target, fired at it with a shotgun but missed. It landed on houses at the junction of South Milton Street and Home Sweet Home Terrace, destroying the post office and killing five people and injuring four, one of whom died in hospital a few days later. Next morning four bombs were dropped in the area of Morice Square and Marlborough Street, Devonport. A butcher was killed when his shop was hit, and three others were seriously injured. These raids continued for the next few weeks, often aimed at selective targets including RAF Mount Batten, the dockyard, North Road Station, and public utilities such as the gas and electricity works. Several houses were destroyed in Goschen Street and Hamilton Street, Keyham Barton, in an afternoon raid on 25 August, and two days later another raid killed twelve inmates and staff of Ford House in Wolseley Road.

Families then began to leave Plymouth for the safer towns and villages of Devon and Cornwall. This evacuation later became official, and at one stage the population fell from around 220,000 in 1939 to 127,000. (According to the official census figures, in 1931 the figure for Plymouth was 227,631, no census was held in 1941 because of the war, and in 1951 it was 208,985.) Arrangements for emergency provisions and housing were hastily made, but ironically most of the premises which had been designated thus were close to target areas and therefore frequently destroyed or damaged themselves, with the result that somewhere else had to be found quickly. The War Office in Whitehall gave little assistance, as officials were apparently reluctant to acknowledge that Plymouth was at risk from bombing, despite the strategic importance of the dockyard and its status as the largest city in England west of Bristol. Local government was inevitably hampered by the loss of records and the repeated destruction of offices, and enlistment depleted the number of civic employees. Early protection facilities for the general public were inadequate, while many of the initial shelters were small and easily flooded.

Anderson shelters were made free to households with an income of less than £250 per year, while those on higher incomes had to purchase them for £7 each.

In July 1940 the Luftwaffe increased its minelaying activities in British coastal waters. These required very accurate navigation, flying at low speed and low altitude. Plymouth was one of the most significant ports which the Luftwaffe was attempting to seal off by laying mines across the harbours. On the night of 22 July four German aircraft, each carrying two magnetic mines, approached the city to lay mines at the Breakwater in Plymouth Sound. One flew into a barrage balloon, went out of control and flew upside down overland, but managed to right itself and accomplish its mission. That same night two or three Nazi aeroplanes were brought down by anti-aircraft guns before they could discharge any of their bombs. They were caught in searchlights as shrapnel burst around them, at least two nosedived, and it was later confirmed that at least one had crashed.

These bombs gradually increased in size, with new landmines being dropped by parachute. The first incendiary attack came on 28 November 1940 when an enemy aircraft dropped four flares over the Turnchapel and Mount Batten district, and several thousand landmines, as well as 100 tons of bombs. Almost at once one of the hangars at RAF Mount Batten was set alight by a high explosive bomb, and a Sunderland flying boat was destroyed. Within a short while another bomber, while aiming for the Air Station, achieved a direct hit on an oil tank in the nearby Admiralty Oil Fuel Depot, adjacent to Turnchapel Railway Station, starting a major conflagration. At Oreston ten people were killed, and four houses were demolished. As the fires around the tanks continued into the next day, two men from the Auxiliary Fire Service were killed and four others were injured. An explosion resulted in a shower of blazing oil on the railway station, and the adjacent buildings immediately caught fire. The flames burnt fiercely until they were finally put out on 1 December. Throughout Plymouth, everyone went in dread of further indiscriminate bombing attacks in any area of the city, and there was a mass evacuation from Turnchapel to Plympton.

Over a hundred enemy bombers had taken part in the raid. The first incendiaries were reasonably small and could be kept under control to some extent with water and sand from individuals, but the later explosive and non-explosive types included delayed firing devices that still burnt while being tackled. Both the Plymouth and Stonehouse Gas Company and the Plymouth Corporation Electricity Works were hit during one attack, and for a brief period Plymouth had no electrical power anywhere in the city. Local gas supplies were vulnerable to persistent disruption, and there were a number of tragic accidents in the course of repair work. Hundreds of houses were destroyed, and the Emergency Committee had the additional responsibility of feeding and housing the homeless. The council provided food and shelter for two days, and after that people were billeted in private houses, with an allowance of 5s for each adult and 3s for each child allotted to the hosts.

An unofficial truce was observed by both sides over Christmas, but it did not last long. In another raid on the evening of 29 December, fourteen high-explosive bombs and about a thousand incendiaries were dropped on the city. About a dozen of the former missed their target and fell into Plymouth Sound, but parts of the Barbican, Cobourg Street and Mutley Plain, and the two main city hospitals, were all hit. Eleven people were killed and twelve seriously injured, while seventeen houses were demolished and about 300 were badly damaged. By midnight the fires were under control, though a few were still smouldering at dawn.

From then, there would be no let-up over the city for more than a few days at a time. On 10 January 1941 a large bomb probably intended for the dockyard fell about 300 yards away on the edge of Devonport Park in front of Portland Place. One man was seriously injured and died later in hospital, while another nine were also injured, and twenty houses were badly damaged. On the next day, a 9ft unexploded bomb dropped during the raid just after Christmas was removed by the bomb disposal squad from Wolsdon Street. Had it gone off, the damage would have been devastating.

Further raids during the next eight weeks claimed more lives, with even larger numbers injured and several buildings demolished. One of the worst was on 13 February, when raiders returning after attacks on Cardiff and Liverpool unloaded additional bombs on Plymouth at around 4.00 a.m. At Alfred Road, Ford, three houses were demolished, and eleven people were trapped in their beds, standing no chance of survival after being buried under several tons of debris. One man had an astonishing escape, surviving unharmed even though a complete side of his house fell away. Also in the same series of raids, two bombs fell next to the Royal Eye Infirmary at Mutley, but failed to explode. Patients and nearby residents were evacuated while the devices were removed.

Not everybody in Plymouth was united against the enemy, and people were occasionally less than discreet in making their feelings known. On 17 March Petty Officer William Johns and his wife Rosalina, of Compton Park Villas Road, were charged with making statements concerning the war likely to cause despondency and alarm. It was alleged that while in an air-raid shelter, Mrs Johns had asked other people taking similar refuge why they were putting up with the war. 'You have no need to stand for it,' she was alleged to have said. 'Why don't wives get their husbands together and persuade them to stop making munitions? Hitler will come in the end and we should welcome

Millbay Station at the east end, next to two bomb craters after an attack in February 1941 in which the Continental Hotel was badly damaged. (Derek Tait)

him with outstretched arms. England has spread filth and lust in every country she has dominated.' Johns supported his wife, adding that everything she said was true, while the navy 'was rotten and has done nothing.' In court he denied ever having made such a statement about the service, while his wife said that most of the evidence for the prosecution was false, that she was speaking from a religious point of view and believed that men ought to stop making munitions. Telling them that their utterances were exceedingly foolish, but that he did not believe there had been any malicious intent behind them, the Chairman of the Bench fined them both £5.

On 20 March 1941 King George VI and Queen Elizabeth paid a visit to Plymouth lasting about seven hours. The royal train arrived at Millbay Station at 10.30 a.m., where a welcoming committee including Lord and Lady Astor, the Australian Prime Minister, Robert Menzies, who was staying with them for a few days, and a contingent of senior naval officers was lined up to greet them. After an official reception the royal entourage were driven to Devonport Dockyard, and showed great interest in the work being done by women on aluminium-cutting machines in one of the workshops. The king inspected Civil Defence and Home Guard units at Guildhall Square, and talked to many local people, including a contingent of men from the minesweepers and patrol vessels.

Meanwhile the queen visited one of the heavily bombed areas and talked to some of the homeless. She remarked to a warden that, 'it is only by keeping our chins up, as we are doing, that we shall win the war.' The king and queen paid a joint visit to the Virginia House Settlement, being used as a food and rest centre for people who had lost their homes in the bombing, where the king in his admiral's uniform sat between Lady Astor and the queen as the mothers sang 'All the Nice Girls Love a Sailor', and then put on a special dancing display. When one woman invited Their Majesties to join in, the king replied, 'We should love to, but we haven't time.' As their visit drew to a close, the queen stood on Plymouth Hoe, looking out to sea, and remarked how peaceful it all looked. They left from Millbay at about 5.30 p.m.

By this time Plymouth had been subjected to eight months of intermittent air raids, but the real devastation was to come all too soon. That same day rumours had been circulating around the Royal Air Force operational room at St Eval, Cornwall, that Plymouth 'was due to catch a packet tonight'.

4

THE
BLITZ

Just three hours after the royal train departed, the air-raid siren sounded an alert. It was soon followed by the sound of anti-aircraft fire, and at 8.39 p.m. an attack started from a group of Heinkel III bombers flying at between 9,900ft and 11,500ft above the city, dropping thirty-four delayed-action high-explosive bombs. The pathfinder force, which should have arrived first and dropped coloured flares to identify selected target areas, arrived at 8.41 p.m., flying at an altitude of 19,000ft. Their shower of flares was followed by 12,500 incendiaries and other high-explosive bombs. After they turned away to go back to their airfields in France, two further squadrons dropped more, including seventeen blockbusters. In addition a squadron sent to bomb the Westland Aircraft Works, Yeovil, diverted to shower bombs on Plymouth after bad weather prevented them from attacking their original target.

That evening a reception was held at the Royal Naval Engineering College, Keyham, for those who had officiated at the royal visit. One of the Wrens was serving a glass of wine to Lord Louis Mountbatten, when they heard a loud rumbling noise. Not realising what it was at first, a friend called out jokingly that an officer had fallen downstairs. Almost at once a naval officer appeared, telling them that the city was under attack. The reception stopped, and the guests, including Lady Astor and Lord Mountbatten, left in an orderly fashion as soon as possible. All the naval personnel present were ordered to report to Stonehouse Town Hall.

During this raid the first to suffer was Spooners, across the road from St Andrew's church. Flames were spreading so fast that the city's own fire brigade could not contain the situation. Within thirty minutes an urgent call went out to other fire brigades all over the West Country asking for assistance, and this was soon extended to cities and towns as far away as Birmingham, Bristol, Swindon and Salisbury. Members of one fire service coming from the latter district said they had no need to ask any directions, as the tremendous glow in the sky was their signpost towards Plymouth. Damage to the water mains meant that most of the supply to the city centre was cut, so water-relay systems were devised and water-carrying vehicles were put into operation. At the barracks, soldiers and naval ratings rushed over twenty pumps from their own establishments to help the fire brigade. Two lines were laid from Sutton Harbour to the Guildhall area, in order to feed into a 20,000 gallon tank.

The Royal Hotel and General Post Office in Westwell Street were next to be destroyed, while the Municipal Offices and Guildhall also sustained damage, as did properties in Millbay, Stonehouse, Union Street and the Octagon. The illumination from these fires made it easier for a second wave of planes to bomb an area of the town extending almost from Stonehouse to Mutley and Cattedown.

When the bombing began many people were away from their homes, having gone to visit friends or spend the evening at the cinema or the dance hall. During a show by the Billy Cotton Band at the Palace Theatre, the manager walked on stage to inform the audience of the air raid in progress. The band continued to play, until a deafening explosion extinguished every light in the theatre. Many in the audience were terrified, but order was maintained as improvised lighting was produced, and the spotlight shone on a lone trumpeter who began

Stonehouse Bridge, barely recognisable after being bombed. (Derek Tait)

to play a solo which immediately produced a calming effect. A factory adjoining the back of the theatre had been hit, and only a backstage safety fire curtain prevented the fire from spreading. Naturally this was kept from members of the audience, who were persuaded to stay until about 5.30 next morning as the streets were not safe. Cotton and his band returned for another show at the same venue the following night, to find just eight in the audience.

In the space of less than three hours that first evening, some 125 enemy aircraft brought terror to the city, and by around midnight the centre of Plymouth was aflame. When the other fire brigades arrived, their sole navigational aid being the bright orange glow in the night sky which indicated where Plymouth was, they found they could only be of limited help with putting out fires because their equipment was not compatible with fire-fighting devices already being used in the city, and had to rely on what hoses they could connect up to the ordinary water mains. As one of them remarked, it was 'like trying to put out a blazing warehouse with a stirrup-pump,' and many fires had to be left to burn themselves out. They were eventually declared under control at about 4.30 a.m., by which time nearly 800 firemen were on duty.

Costers, Frankfort Street, a clothing and general department store known particularly as a supplier of school clothing, after the bombing of March 1941. (Derek Tait)

Firemen hosing down the *Western Morning News* office, to prevent the fire from spreading. Adjacent to Costers, it had recently been built using newer materials, and was one of the few buildings to survive with the exterior intact. (Derek Tait)

That night alone 336 people were killed. Among them were four nurses, three aged between 16 and 19, working at the City Hospital Maternity Ward. Nineteen babies and children in the ward, and two mothers, were also among the fatalities. It had been the enemy's intention to destroy the business centre and, in the words of historian Pat Twyford (a war correspondent on the editorial staff of the paper, and later author of *It Came to our Door*, a detailed account of the city's wartime experiences), 'Plymouth's heart was torn out and mauled.'

At 7.00 next morning the BBC radio news bulletin announced in its main story that a town in the south-west had been the main target of last night's German raids, with two churches, a cinema and many houses hit, but details of the damage done or casualties inflicted were not yet available. The number of bombers involved was comparatively small, and the attack had ceased before midnight. Only from the 1.00 p.m. bulletin onwards was Plymouth mentioned by name. It was generally felt that the BBC had deliberately downplayed the seriousness of the raids in order to prevent what might otherwise have been seen as a propaganda gift to the enemy, after the heavy bombing of London and Coventry. Nevertheless many Plymothians resented this, as they considered that the media had made light of their sufferings to the public.

City Hospital, Maternity Ward, another early casualty of the Blitz. (Derek Tait)

Derry's Clock after the bombing of 20 March 1941. On the right The Bank Chambers, now The Bank Public House, survived, as did the basic structure of Derry's Clock, though not the clock faces. (Derek Tait)

George Street after the bombing. (Derek Tait)

Tavistock Street off Fore Street in Devonport, with the Alhambra Theatre on the right.
(Derek Tait)

Drake Circus and the Guinness clock. (Derek Tait)

Leigham Street, adjoining Citadel Road, the Hoe, after being bombed. (Derek Tait)

The remains of Cornwall Street, with signs for two businesses directing customers to new temporary locations. (Derek Tait)

The carnage inflicted the following night, 21 March, was even worse, with such fierce heat from the fires that plate glass melted and asphalt roadways turned to liquid. At about 8.50 p.m. it started once again without warning, when the sudden appearance of raiders coming in from the north-east caught the city by surprise. This time the target was the area adjoining the one hit the previous night, and pathfinder planes encircled Plymouth for about twenty minutes as they positioned themselves before dropping their flares on the chosen spot. Bombers soon followed, encountering little if any resistance from the Royal Air Force. Fires soon ranged over a wide region, from the timber yards and tar distillery at Coxside in the east to the Royal Naval Barracks at Keyham and the Royal William Victualling Yard in the west. One man was killed and two were injured on Drake's Island. St Andrew's church was burnt out, losing its roof and windows, with only the walls and tower still standing. The Guildhall and the Municipal Offices, which had also been fortunate to escape the previous night, were gutted, with only burnt-out shells remaining. The Westminster and Hacker's hotels in the Crescent, and the Plymouth Co-operative store, were razed to the ground. The bus depot at Milehouse was almost obliterated, with one bus literally thrown onto the roof of the main shed by the force of the explosions, and fifty other vehicles destroyed. Derry's Clock Tower remained standing, but the clock faces were broken by flying debris.

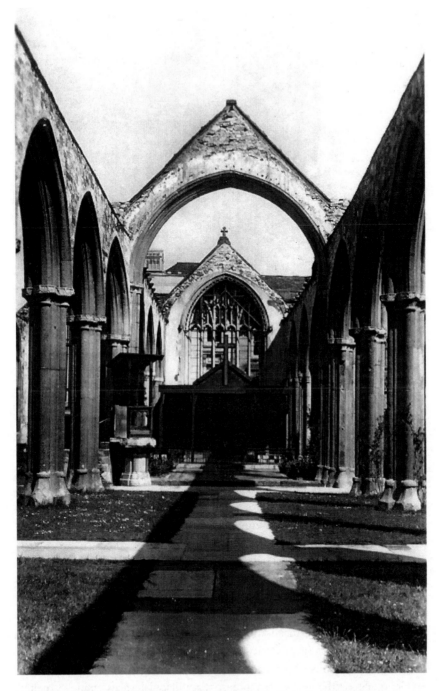

St Andrew's church, which had lost nearly all its roof after being bombed. The main chancel became a garden until rebuilding, with flowers planted around the pillars. (Derek Tait)

Charles church, which had stood in Vennel Street until the area was badly bombed. In June 1953 the Reconstruction Committee proposed to demolish the ruins but it was decided to preserve them as a war memorial. (Derek Tait)

Many churches were burnt out, including King Street Wesleyan church and the Baptist church in George Street. The shell of Charles church, which had stood unscathed for almost 300 years, would later be preserved as a memorial to those who had lost their lives. The Hoe Pier, Hoe Café and Hoe Grammar School, the Prince of Wales Hospital, and the Royal Sailors' Rest all suffered a similar fate. As there was no city centre left for the buses to serve, the Western National Omnibus Company moved its terminus from St Andrew's Cross to Sherwell Arcade, close to the City Museum in Tavistock Road.

By the morning of 22 March, the only buildings still undamaged in the city centre were the National Westminster Bank in Bedford Street and the *Western Morning News* office in Frankfort Street. Providentially both had been constructed only a few years earlier from fire-resistant materials. The newspaper's storage area which housed the photographic collection was destroyed, resulting in the loss to posterity of a unique photographic archive which comprised thousands of irreplaceable prints and negatives of old Plymouth. In George Street the heat was so intense that thick plate-glass windows melted, gold in a jeweller's shop turned to liquid and trickled away, and tins of meat and soup packed together in a food shop exploded, fusing into lumps of molten tin.

A policeman inspecting bomb damage in Union Street. (Derek Tait)

The view from St Andrew's church looking towards Charles church. Most old buildings at the top of Old Town Street were later demolished to make way for the new main post office, while the area on the right became St Andrew's Cross roundabout. (Derek Tait)

Apart from the bank, the shopping thoroughfare of Bedford Street was reduced to a heap of ruins. Every section of the civil defence organisation rose to the occasion, and the first aid and rescue services treated hundreds of casualties. One of the most important bodies was the Women's Voluntary Service, founded in 1938, with an office in George Street, which became the Women's Voluntary Service for Civil Defence, or the WVS. Its members assisted with evacuating families from bombed premises and making medical supplies such as bandages from old sheets, pyjamas and nursing gowns.

Those who were involved in civil defence frequently worked at no little personal danger to themselves. A bomb-disposal squad had removed one heavy device at Osborne Place, the Hoe, and were about to drive it away on a lorry when it exploded, killing all five men as well as destroying the vehicle. One man in an adjoining street, about to get into his car, was also killed in the blast.

Local solicitor John Foot, of the well-established local firm Foot & Bowden, wrote to his wife Anne to tell her of the destruction of their office in Lockyer Street and subsequent loss of their papers. His father Isaac, he said, had received a call at 4.00 a.m. to tell him that his business premises were on fire. On asking if there was anything he could do, he was told there was not, so he said he might as well go back to bed again, and he did, sleeping until 9.00 a.m.

A bomb disposal squad at work removing an unexploded device. (Derek Tait)

'I think everybody's been made a bit lightheaded by the enormity of the blow at Plymouth. You walk down the street and see old gentlemen surveying the wreckage of their businesses and cracking jokes with the rest who're in the same plight.'

In just two nights of bombing, the shopping centre of Plymouth had been obliterated. Nearly all thoroughfares were blocked by debris or bomb craters, and were subsequently closed to traffic. Demolition squads moved in, charged with the task of bringing down the shells of burnt-out buildings, with walls in a precarious state and posing considerable danger. Among those which had to be destroyed and thus made safe was the Co-operative Society building in Frankfort Gate. A fighter airfield using large amounts of rubble from the destruction of Plymouth to build the runways was constructed at Yelverton, and opened for use on 15 August 1941.

Large collections of furniture, including many fine pianos, were removed from damaged houses and required storage. Accommodation was found for large items in bandstands at Home Park, which was considered relatively safe as it was on the outskirts of the city, and carefully labelled until they could be returned to their owners. Yet even Home Park was not immune, and much was destroyed in further raids only a few weeks later.

A couple saving what they could from their bombed house. Sheets and blankets were in particularly short supply after so many shops' stocks had been destroyed. (Derek Tait)

Collecting salvage from a bombed home in aid of the war effort. (Derek Tait)

Plymouth Argyle's ground, Home Park, was mistakenly thought to be safe from the bombing. Furniture and pianos were stored here until destroyed in a raid in April 1941. (Derek Tait)

Early in April, Lady Astor broadcast a short message about the effect of enemy action on Plymouth to listeners in America, telling them that three hours after Their Majesties had left, 'Hitler's New Order had arrived.' To the people of Plymouth, she broadcast that, 'Mercifully we have suffered only half of what Hitler's other victims have suffered. At least we have not been driven out of our country. Our sailors, soldiers and airmen will see that we never do.'

As April progressed there were only a few days and nights of respite, before further alerts and raids came. The worst of these was on the night of 22 April, resulting in the destruction of the Air Raid Precaution's control centre beneath Devonport Market and an attack on Devonport Telephone Exchange. Devonport had naturally been a prime target because of the dockyard, and although it had been spared the worst of the damage the previous month, now its shopping centre was also virtually gone. Only two badly damaged stores, Marks & Spencer and Burton's, were left standing, and what was left of them was eventually razed to the ground in favour of dockyard extensions.

One structure which was fortunate to survive was the railway bridge which spanned Pennycomequick Hill. A bomb missed it by only a few feet,

Navy personnel, sorting salvaged items into separate containers for paper, iron and rags. (Derek Tait)

Devonport Station, 30 April 1941, with debris strewn across the tracks, and a heavily bombed house on the right. (Derek Tait)

The Millbay Laundry, Stonehouse, a target area because of the railway station and docks. (Derek Tait)

although it left a large crater in the road immediately below. It was fortunate that all the city's railways, bridges and viaducts likewise escaped damage.

The death toll for March and April was estimated at 926 but the actual figure was undoubtedly more, as some records of known deaths were destroyed in subsequent raids. When whole families were wiped out, there was often nobody left to identify the dead, thus accounting for many of the 'missing' statistics. Naval ratings from HMS *Raleigh* at Torpoint were called upon to assist with the grim task of recovering bodies from the ruins and the Corporation cart collected up human remains after each bombing attack. These remains were placed in sandbags, labelled and sent to city mortuaries to await identification if possible. Such macabre details were never reported in contemporary newspapers, and it was left to historians to record them many years after the event. The task of overseeing such appalling but necessary duties was the responsibility of Percy Cole, who was ironically also the Corporation entertainments manager.

The worst disasters in terms of lives lost at this time were when a bomb at the Royal Naval Barracks destroyed a petty officers' block, killing about eighty people, and an air-raid shelter at Portland Square, opposite the City Museum, was also hit, leaving seventy-two dead. The Most Holy Redeemer Roman

The Western National Bus Depot at Prince Rock, after an attack on 30 April 1944 in which three men were killed and sixteen others seriously injured. (Derek Tait)

Catholic church at Keyham was destroyed, and the Astors' home near the Hoe, No. 3 Eliot Terrace, was damaged. In another raid, some 72,000 books were destroyed in a fire at the Central Library in Tavistock Road, including 41,000 in the lending library, 16,000 in the reference department and the Devon and Cornwall Collection of 15,000 books. Fortunately about 5,000 volumes were out on loan and most of these remained safe. Some stock on the shelves was salvaged, but it was mainly thanks to the general public's donation of around 4,500 books and Isaac Foot's generous presentation of several thousand from his own library that the service could start again so quickly after such a disaster. On 8 August the lord mayor reopened the lending library on a temporary basis in the museum part of the building, which had miraculously remained unscathed. The Proprietary Library in Cornwall Street similarly lost several hundred priceless volumes. Also badly damaged was the Athenaeum, where the Plymouth Institution had housed its irreplaceable antiquarian collections.

André Savignon, a French author and journalist who was in the city at the height of the Blitz, later wrote in stark terms of the devastation around him:

> Any description would be too trivial. The town has had its stomach ripped open and we are paddling in its guts … Ashes, mud, dust – my eyes are smarting – and above all this poignant acrid smell, this cold smell – yes, that's it, cold: this effluvia of death that even the wind from the sea does not succeed in chasing away and which wavers to and fro, as though hooked to the ruins.

Groups of servicemen were sent to help salvage stock from bombed shop premises, entering each damaged business in turn, reclaiming everything worth salvaging and laying it out on tarpaulin sheets for owners to examine what had been saved and assess what had been destroyed.

Even animals were enlisted to help and search for the missing of their own kind in the war effort. The People's Dispensary for Sick Animals, which had been founded in 1917 to provide care for animals whose owners could not afford their vet's bills, had its own animal rescue squad that worked with Civil Defence Workers. Many animals were trapped and injured during the Blitz, and dogs were used to find them. Some were awarded the Dicken Medal which the press dubbed 'The Animals' VC'.

The victims of the April raids were buried at Efford cemetery in a mass grave on the afternoon of 28 April. Each coffin was draped with a Union Flag and floral tributes ranging from humble posies of primroses to official wreaths and crosses. Those who took part in the service included the Bishop of Exeter,

The navy helping to move salvaged furniture and belongings. (Derek Tait)

The Animal Rescue Squad at work during the Blitz. (Derek Tait)

The mass grave at Efford, where victims of the raids of April 1941 were buried. (Derek Tait)

the Bishop of Plymouth, the Roman Catholic Bishop of Plymouth and the Revd W.D. Campbell representing the Nonconformist congregations. Representatives from the Salvation Army and officers from the armed services also attended.

At an orphanage, the children aged between 7 and 13 were fast asleep when one of the raids began. They were woken, told to take their pillows and blankets with them, and ushered out into an underground shelter. Once installed there, the matron was amused to see them making a game by hiding their heads under the blankets at the sound of every new explosion. When it was over and the all-clear was sounded, she suggested they ought to sing something. They immediately broke into 'There'll always be an England'.

While Plymouth was recovering from the worst of the war damage, the centre was cordoned off. Main roads were guarded by armed soldiers and policemen, and soldiers were also stationed in railway signal boxes, with the objective of protecting the place from spectators from Devon and Cornwall who evidently had nothing better than to come and see the ruins as if they were some kind of tourist attraction. Those who came to look before the cordon was in place caused considerable resentment among those who had suffered. Salvaged timber was stacked in streets of empty houses, until it was realised that this created a new danger in itself. This was too close to the dockyard, and if there were further air raids, the timber would surely catch fire. The dockyard might be destroyed, and the fires would act as beacons for the enemy bomber crews.

The guards also found it necessary to keep a watch on properties and try to prevent any looting, as there were always a few youthful opportunists around who could not resist the temptation of petty theft. In April a young sailor was fined £2 at Plymouth Juvenile Court for taking a quantity of chocolate and a number of regimental badges from premises which had been damaged by bombing. In sentencing him, the chairman warned that others had been sent to prison for similar crimes. Two schoolboys under 12 years of age were brought before the magistrates after a policeman had caught them smashing windows, banisters and cupboards with an iron bar in an unoccupied house at Stonehouse. Their excuse was that they had wanted to obtain some firewood to take home to their mothers. They were bound over for twelve months. A 14-year-old errand boy who had left school was charged with stealing a collecting box containing £3 from a house in Bainbridge Avenue. He said he knew the lady who lived there was out and the scullery window was not bolted. As a result he was ordered to return to school, and bound over for

A barrage balloon crew clearing away the remains of the bandstand for salvage and sorting out anything that could be salvaged for the war effort. (Derek Tait)

Two boys looking at bomb damage at Turnchapel. (Derek Tait)

eighteen months. The courts also had to deal with several infringements of blackout regulations, generally imposing a fine of £2 for a first offence and more for those who re-offended.

Another unfortunate case, very much a sign of the times, was heard towards the end of the war. A young war widow of Barne Road, St Budeaux, with three children aged between 2 and 11, was dependent on a 'very small pension' of £2 9s per week. She supplemented this by going into prostitution, sometimes bringing customers back to her flat. One Christmas Eve and Christmas Day she left the children on their own, without food or money to buy any, though they would probably have been unable to find shops open during the holiday season even if she had given them something. They had to go and beg from their neighbours, who promptly reported the mother for neglecting them. Despite warnings from the National Society for the Prevention of Cruelty to Children she continued to ply her trade, although she paid people to keep an eye on the youngsters. However, the babysitters turned out to be 'undesirable characters', and attempts to have her pension increased were turned down because of her way of life. When the flat was inspected it was found to contain very little bedding or furniture. An application was made by the NSPCC and the children were taken into care.

In March 1941 the Essential Work (General Provisions) Order required all skilled workers to register in order to make sure that essential jobs were filled as far as possible. Three years later Muriel Jones, a 24-year-old bus conductress employed by Plymouth Corporation, came up before the magistrates after not having turned up for her job for fifty-six days in 1943 and ten days in 1944. Her plea that she found it hard to get up was not accepted, and she was fined £5 for being absent from work under the terms of the Order.

After the raid on 28 April 1941, Mr A. Titherley, senior regional officer of the Ministry of Health, met the city's Emergency Committee and agreed that a large part of Plymouth should be declared an evacuation area. The evacuation would be achieved in stages with certain areas scheduled for moving people away at first.

By the beginning of May, Plymouth was benefiting from a short respite. However, there was a problem with the weather and, as it became wet, the dust became black mud. It made clearance work more difficult, and many of the thoroughfares were still completely blocked.

Winston Churchill, accompanied by his wife Clementine, visited Plymouth on 2 May. As Lord Astor was ill, they were met and entertained by Lady Astor,

Winston Churchill touring Plymouth on 2 May 1941, with his wife Clementine seated on his right. (Derek Tait)

who took them round the naval establishments. Although they were both of
the same party, the Prime Minister and the Member for Plymouth Sutton
had already had several sharp exchanges on various subjects in the House of
Commons, and even in wartime they would be in less than total agreement.
On arrival Churchill had insisted that he wanted his wife to accompany him
to all public meetings in the city, but Lady Astor told him that the programme
could not be altered at such short notice. After a few moments of reflection,
he went for a short stroll. On his return, he told her that all supreme decisions
would be made by him alone, and therefore Mrs Churchill would come
too. They visited quays and workshops at the dockyard, inspected warships,
were invited to lunch, and then Churchill went to Admiralty House for his
customary short nap before they toured the heavily blitzed areas in a large
open Daimler.

As the Churchills' vehicle was driven around the city, a police car drove on
ahead, announcing his presence through a loudspeaker. They stopped twice so
he could exchange a few words with the crowds who were lining the route.
Unlike the tours he had previously made of other blitzed cities, he did not get
out and walk. When he was visibly moved to tears, taking his hat off and saying,
'God bless you,' to them, Lady Astor snapped in full hearing of others that it
was all very well for him to cry, 'but you've got to do something!' At Guildhall
Square he watched men engaged in demolishing the more dangerous
structures, and somebody shouted out, 'What about Berlin?' 'We are giving
it them more every day,' he answered at once. Before he left, he remarked
that their houses may be low but their hearts were high, while Mrs Churchill
told a group of women outside the Astors' house that she thought 'the way
you have stood up to all this is simply marvellous.' Their visit resulted in a
temporary lifting of morale, but otherwise it produced no immediate results.
As Lady Astor wrote a few days later to the Countess of Halifax, wife of the
British Ambassador to the United States, 'It was a moving sight, but why it has
not moved him [Churchill] to action I cannot understand.'

Double summer time was introduced on 4 May 1941, thus putting the
United Kingdom two hours ahead of Greenwich Mean Time. This had the
effect of shortening Plymouth's blackout period and giving an extra hour of
daylight for clearing operations on the city streets which were strewn with
glass, timber and debris, and riddled with bomb craters. Tradespeople making
deliveries in motor vehicles had to put up with the regular inconvenience of
sudden punctures.

By the first week of the month, seventy-one Plymouth firefighters were on
the sick list, mostly through exhaustion. Arrangements were made to bring
in an extra hundred firemen from Wales as a temporary measure. Many civil

defence workers needed a sustained period of rest for the same reason, and an exchange of personnel was arranged with others outside Plymouth to allow them some respite. At around the same time there was thankfully a lull in the air raids. Germany was preparing for the invasion of Russia, the Luftwaffe units based in northern France which had been instrumental in the Blitz were transferred to the eastern European front, and German bombers were now flown by less experienced crews.

Between 6 and 17 May there were seven further nights on which residential areas of Plymouth experienced raids, but the tally of death and destruction was on a far lesser scale. People at sea were not immune, and in June it was revealed that two fishermen had been killed when their boat was attacked by a volley of bullets from German aircraft. They had no means of protecting themselves and they were subsequently found dead when their vessel drifted back to shore.

Within the last few weeks, the city centre had been brutally altered beyond recognition. The pre-war skyline had disappeared, never to return. Civil and government offices, and their relevant records and files, had been destroyed, thus causing innumerable administration difficulties. Temporary offices scattered throughout the city had to be set up to deal with the day-to-day business of issuing important documents, permits, coupons, money allowances and the like. Houses which had not been damaged were sometimes still deprived of essential supplies, and families often had to be evacuated because of the danger from unexploded bombs nearby. Gas and electricity supplies were cut off, leaving people reliant on candlelight after dark, while water supplies were polluted and had to be boiled before drinking. Not everybody was fortunate enough to have running water, which in some streets gushed out of smashed wells, damaged sewers and pipes.

Meanwhile, men in the armed forces applied for compassionate leave after hearing of the devastation in their home city, and many returned to an alien townscape, to find their homes gone and some or all of their family dead. One particularly tragic case was that of Corporal Albert Davies of the Devon Regiment, who had been stationed away from the city. When he received a telegram to inform him of bad news at home, his comrades had a whip-round to provide him with the train fare back. On his arrival, he made a point of passing by the shelter where he knew his 32-year-old wife and six children, aged between 14 years and 2 months, always went during the raids. All that remained was a mass of rubble. When he reached his sister's house at Mount Gould, she had to give him the heartbreaking news that they had all perished. Plymouth, he decided, would no longer be his home. He told her he had applied to be drafted for service overseas, and he did not intend to return.

An equally sad episode was that of John Bartlett, a small boy who had walked out of the cinema one night in March to find the city ablaze. Next month he was dug out of the Anderson shelter in the back garden of his parents' home at Swilly. Suffering from head injuries and broken ribs, he was taken by stretcher to an ambulance, while his mother lay in the garden gasping for breath. From hospital in Plymouth he was taken by train to Truro, then to hospital in Birmingham where he lay in bed for three months, waiting for his parents to come and visit him. One day the ward sister took him aside and told him that he would have to be brave in view of what she was going to tell him. Only then did he learn that they had been killed in the explosion. He also chose never to live in, or even go back to, his home city again.

Shelters were never totally safe from the ferocity of the warfare waged overhead on innocent citizens. In another instance that same month, a woman warden had to report to the Air Raid Precautions staff the tragic news that her husband, son and brother-in-law had all been killed together. Her husband, who had also been a warden, had ushered them all into a private shelter just before a bomb fell on them.

Housing problems in the immediate aftermath of the Blitz caused frequent difficulties for the authorities. A letter dated 5 June was sent to Lord Astor from four Plymouth residents who had had to be moved when their houses were destroyed and were temporarily, none too happily, at the Public Assistance Institution in Redruth:

I am appealing on behalf of the undersigned evacuees of Plymouth. We are residing at the above address being sent by the Billeting Authorities at Plymouth. We have no money and we cannot get help from any source, we all want a change of clothes and we want footwear. We have been at this Institution for a period of 5 weeks. We have interviewed the Billeting Officer of Redruth and Camborne they cannot give us any information regarding what is going to happen to us, they simply tell us Plymouth Authorities are responsible for us.

We are all inhabitants of Plymouth and have lost our home by means of enemy action we should be very grateful to you if we could receive some financial help or information regarding what is going to happen to us all. We were evacuated from the City Hospital on the 5th May, not knowing we were being sent to a Workhouse.

We are billeted in a hut with inmates and mental patients and I think you will agree with us being inhabitants of Plymouth we don't deserve this treatment. If you could help us with some money to get necessary clothing and footwear we should be very grateful.

The writer was Frank Thorning, a single man of 39 who had suffered from debility since a serious operation four years earlier, and whose house at Portland Villas had been demolished. Lord Astor forwarded it to the Town Clerk's Office with a covering letter, reporting that Thorning had previously been in receipt of 12s weekly relief from Plymouth, and 8s 3d National Health Insurance benefit. He had also been given £3 by the Assistance Board to replace his lost clothing, but they could not award him a weekly allowance as he was being wholly maintained in the Rest Centre. 'It would be advisable,' Astor's letter concluded, 'for other accommodation to be found for this man at an early date as he is inclined to air his grievances and cause trouble with the other persons in the Rest Centre.' Arrangements were made for the three eldest of the men to return to Plymouth very shortly, with the remainder being billeted as soon as possible.

Less than four weeks later, on 1 July, Councillor Townsend wrote to the Town Clerk with regard to another issue which he had been asked to investigate:

Does the Emergency Committee know of the anomaly that seems to prevail regarding re-housing of bombed out people in Plymouth? It came to my notice yesterday that although the Housing Committee has vacant properties that could be tenanted, people who are billeted outside the City cannot be brought back as tenants for those houses by the billeting officer, because the 'housing authority' reserve the right to keep them empty without any regard to the general billeting requirements of the billeting officer. Surely there should be some collaboration! What does the Emergency Committee think of this situation?

This prompted a letter the following day from the clerk to his Housing Estates Manager, regarding the allegation 'that homeless persons cannot be housed in Corporation property. I presume there is no truth in Councillor Townsend's statement. Please confirm.' The manager was able to assure him that Townsend had indeed been misinformed.

Believing that people would be rather less frightened when part of a large group than when on their own, Lord Astor decided that one good way of raising morale would be to arrange with the council to invite military bands to come and play on the Hoe. On 6 June 1941 a notice appeared in the press, informing people that there would be Cornish Floral dancing to the music of a band at 7.30 the following evening, and the lady mayoress would be present. Several dancing pupils in the city would give a demonstration, and the public would then be invited to take part. Next week a band would play on the Hoe every afternoon and evening. These concerts and dances

Lady Astor dancing with a sailor on the Hoe, summer 1941. (Derek Tait)

became a very popular attraction, with thousands attending and taking part, Lady Astor proving the life and soul of the party and generally leading off the dancing herself.

The playwright Noel Coward, who visited Plymouth as a guest of the Astors in July 1941, wrote approvingly in his diary of watching a crowd consisting of several hundred girls with sailors, soldiers and others; 'a sight so infinitely touching, not that it was consciously brave, but because it was so ordinary and unexhibitionist'. At the same time he thought Plymouth was a pitiful sight; 'houses that held sailor families since the time of Drake spread across the road in rubble and twisted wood.'

As Member of Parliament for Sutton as well as lady mayoress, Lady Astor fought hard to obtain official recognition of Plymouth's plight and government help for the city. She was particularly angry that the House of Commons only debated the Fire Services (Emergency Provisions) Bill later in May, after Plymouth had been devastated by enemy action over several weeks. During the Blitz she became famous for raising morale among the city's servicemen and civilians by performing cartwheels to entertain sailors and small children. She was indefatigable in her efforts to raise spirits among the civilians who were suffering so badly during the conflict. One morning after a particularly heavy raid, she made her way through the rubble and found a young woman aged 22, standing speechless on the spot where her home had stood the night before. Now it was gone, and so were her baby, her mother and her grandmother. Lady Astor put her arm around the woman's shoulder and stood there with her until they moved away together. Throughout the war years she would make a special effort to comfort many others who were so suddenly and tragically bereaved. Although they wished it to be kept private, she and Lord Astor both added codicils to their wills stating that if either of them should be killed in a bombing raid, they wished to be buried in a common grave in Plymouth together with others who had perished in the same way.

Thinking that it might cheer the people up to see a little glamour in their drab lives, Lady Astor once suggested to a visiting admiral that he should accompany her on one of her regular morale-raising perambulations around the ruined city. The consequence of this was not quite what they had expected. She dressed in her best coat and finest pearls, while he was instructed to put on his finest uniform, and they walked through the rubble-strewn streets with a young naval officer in attendance, talking to men, women and children as they went. When they found a side alley that had somehow remained unscathed by the bombing, she walked up to the house at the end and banged on the door. A small girl peered out around a net curtain on the upper floor, looked at them with curiosity, and then disappeared briefly. Moments later she came back, opened the window, and called to them: 'Mam says, if 'tis a sailor, 'e's to put five shillin' in the box by th' door and 'er'll see 'im directly.' All three looked in astonishment at each other, then roared with laughter.

The lull which followed the raids in April and May was too good to last. On the clear moonlit night of 4/5 July, further bombs were dropped on residential areas including Hartley, Keyham, Laira, Crownhill, Beacon Park, and St Budeaux, with eighteen killed and fourteen injured. An explosion on the Hoe killed all members of two families, and the body of one victim was found 300 yards away. Another raid in the Devonport area four nights later left two policemen dead as they sheltered in a doorway in Fore Street and seven people were injured, while eight trapped in the ruins of a demolished house were safely rescued.

On 10 October 1941 a parade of tanks left Mutley Plain for the Octagon, where they went on show to raise funds under the banner of 'Speed the Tanks'. The 25-ton Waltzing Matilda and the two 16-ton Valentine tanks, plus scout cars and breakdown lorries, under the command of Lieutenant F.J. Turpin, appealed to the public, 'for all the tanks you can give both ourselves and the Russians'.

The Hoe Slopes, attacked during a raid on 5 July 1941. (Derek Tait)

In January 1942, in accordance with the provisions of the Emergency Powers (Defence) Acts 1939 and 1940, a start was made in the Mutley area collecting what were deemed the city's least essential railings for iron and steel scrap, though any considered to be of particular historical or ornamental interest would be spared. Owners of affected properties were invited to claim for compensation, and collection was extended to the Compton, Crownhill, St Budeaux, Pennycross and Molesworth wards about a week later. Railings were cut from their bases and gates lifted from their hinges to be taken away to smelting centres. As Twyford noted, 'There was no sentiment in this business; neither was there any option.'

In November 1941 plans were announced for the first of three new villages for evacuees and war service staff to be opened shortly, sponsored by the National Service Hostels Corporation on behalf of the government. These would consist of brick-built accommodation blocks with their own kitchens, electric lighting, a sick bay and their own police stations. The first had provision for 3,000 people, with families accommodated in rooms with four bunks in two tiers and single women in dormitories of twenty bunks. It included three large kitchens and eight 'feeding centres' that could seat up to 330 people at one sitting, looked after by a staff of eighty. Accommodation was free for the first two weeks but thereafter single residents had to pay 5s per week and families were charged double. A rest centre for 320 people was also to be erected on the outskirts of the city.

On 3 March 1942 a number of City of Plymouth police and fire officers attended an investiture at Buckingham Palace, where King George VI presented them with the British Empire Medal for bravery and gallant conduct during the bombing raids of the previous year. On 21 March, the first anniversary of the large air raids, the 19-year-old King Peter of Yugoslavia arrived in Plymouth, and took the salute the following day at the parade which marked the beginning of Plymouth Warship Week. The march past along Tavistock Road was the biggest pageant Plymouth had witnessed since the outbreak of war. The young king had an indirect link with Plymouth in that his great-grandfather Prince Alfred, Duke of Edinburgh, had been Commander-in-Chief at Devonport exactly half a century earlier. Warship Week raised money to build additional merchant ships and warships, with events including exhibitions, concerts at the Palace Theatre, Mutley Methodist Schoolroom, and the British Legion Hall at Crownhill, a ball at the Guildhall, and parades throughout the city. By the end of the week, the target of £1.2 million had been exceeded by over £40,000.

On 23 April a gilt silver cup which had been given to Sir Francis Drake by Queen Elizabeth I was bought at Christie's in London by the National

King George VI and Queen Elizabeth at Guildhall Square, 7 May 1942, on a visit comprising part of a three-day tour of Devon and Cornwall. (Derek Tait)

Arts Collection Fund for £2,100, and it was announced that the cup was to be presented to the City of Plymouth in recognition of the gallantry of its inhabitants. A fortnight later, on 7 May 1942, King George VI and Queen Elizabeth visited the city again. They arrived by car at the city boundary, Plym Bridge Lane, shortly after midday, driving via Milehouse and Camel's Head to Mount Wise. Although they had a programme of separate visits to service establishments, they made joint appearances at the YMCA at Hoe Mansions Hotel, and a civic reception in Abbey Hall. While the king was inspecting a parade of the Royal Marines, one man fell to the ground in a dead faint. None of his comrades batted an eyelid as he was carefully picked up and removed on the orders of the sergeant.

Two months later there was another royal visit. On 11 July the king's youngest brother George, Duke of Kent, President of the RNLI, came attired in the uniform of an Air Commodore, to present awards to members of crew and the coxswain of a lifeboat which had rescued two men from a Sunderland flying boat that had crashed on the coast near Plymouth in January. Tragically the Duke was killed in a similar accident in Scotland in a Sunderland flying boat six weeks later. Among memorial services held for him over the next few days was one at St Catherine's church in Plymouth.

That summer it was reported that tuberculosis was on the increase in Plymouth. At the annual meeting of the Tuberculosis Care and After Care Committee on 26 August, the superintendent of Mount Gould Hospital said that men from the merchant navy were particularly prone to the disease, and sanatoria were being filled. The main reason was that young adults, especially women, were working too long in factories and not getting enough fresh air, and there was a general lowering of resistance through the absence of certain foods.

In the autumn a 21-year-old Plymouth-born merchant navy seaman, Duncan Alexander Scott-Ford, was convicted of selling information to enemy agents on the movement of British shipping. When arrested by the authorities he admitted the offences, and at his trial in October he was found guilty. Asked if there were any grounds for a reprieve, the commandant of the detention centre at which he had been held replied that, 'there may well be many who will agree that death by hanging is almost too good for a sailor who will encompass the death of thousands of his shipmates without qualm.' He was executed at Wandsworth on 3 November. His trial was kept a secret from the press until after his death, when it was reported that he had lost his life after betraying his country for £18, as a warning to others who might be similarly tempted.

5

KEEPING CALM AND CARRYING ON

Despite the devastation of the bombing raids and the large areas which had turned to little more than rubble, valiant efforts were made as far as possible to try and keep up some spirit of normality. Some of the larger city stores, including Dingles, Spooners, Yeo's and Pophams, moved to small, older makeshift shops on the edge of the centre, leaving signs on their old bombed-out premises directing customers to a change of address. Others, including Woolworths, Marks & Spencer, Costers and Boots, took stalls in the pannier market and paid a daily rent of 3*d* per square foot, erected open-air stalls, or set up in smaller premises, in makeshift Nissan huts and even sometimes in residential front rooms. Mutley Plain had remained relatively unscathed, and as the stores' main refuge for a time it became the city's main shopping centre. Apart from the dockyard, the retail industry had been the city's largest employer before 1939. Loss of staff and a fall in the population, and therefore customers, added to the woes of shops trying to recover from the loss of their premises and much of their stock. Many major stores which supplied much of the city's food, clothing and essential supplies such as bedding had lost their stock, thus resulting in a severe shortage of stock which had to be replenished by urgent deliveries from other parts of the country which had suffered less badly. Clothing was rationed from June 1941. People were issued with booklets containing clothing coupons, and were instructed to 'make do and mend' so that clothing factories and their workers could concentrate on giving greater priority to producing munitions.

Plymouth was recognised as an officially protected area, and a stringent watch was kept for enemy aliens. At 9.30 every night a curfew for transport was imposed. Cinemas and theatres remained open, as movie-going was considered

Some major shops and businesses, trading in the pannier market after their main premises were destroyed. (Derek Tait)

A trader operating from a handcart. (Derek Tait)

essential for morale, but they had to close by 9.00 p.m., and public houses by 10.00 p.m., but customers who insisted on remaining until closing time generally had to walk home afterwards because of the lack of public transport. Before the war Plymouth had decided to scrap the tram routes, but some tracks still remained in place, especially on the route through Peverell, and any trams still available were brought back into use.

Identity cards were introduced for adults and children, the former carrying blue cards, the latter cream. If children became separated from their parents or if their houses were bombed, it proved an ideal way for the police to establish their names, and facilitate a safe return to their families.

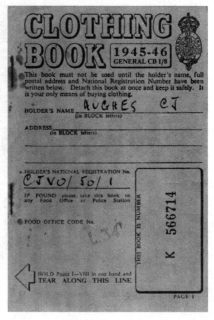

A clothing ration book. (Derek Tait)

The city council took over disused bakeries in Commercial Road and Treville Street in order to provide cooked meals to residents made homeless as a result of the bombing, with retired naval cooks and unemployed bakers providing the service at a rate of 1s 3½d per hour, plus a war bonus of 6s per week and double pay on Sundays. 'Blitz Soup', comprising beans, lentils, peas, carrots and macaroni, was served in restaurants throughout the city.

The refreshments available at places of public entertainment were strictly curtailed. At the end of July 1942 sweets were affected by points rationing. When it was announced that such a measure would be introduced in a few days' time, there were long queues at the confectioners, especially premises in Ebrington Street and Mutley Plain, where they had not yet sold out. One stall in the market had continuous crowds, and the vendor had to ration each customer to 2s 6d worth of chocolate, comprising a dozen blocks. Two months later, cinema patrons could no longer buy ice creams during the interval, and the sale of chocolates was likewise suspended a few months later. Organisations such as the Mercantile Associations of Plymouth and Devonport, the Plymouth Chamber of Commerce, and the Rotary Club continued with their business activities throughout the war years. However, they suspended their annual dinners and other social events, which were not

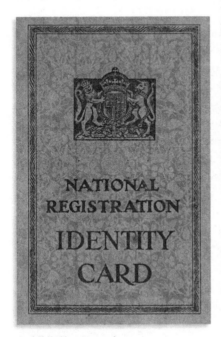

A child's identity card.
(Derek Tait)

A National Registration Identity card for
adults. (Derek Tait)

felt to be in keeping with the wartime spirit when so many other people were
undergoing privations.

Although the dockyards were the principal targets, civilian casualties
were high, and looting of bombed houses was sadly all too frequent. On any
night that a raid was expected – and for many weeks this became a way of
life – tens of thousands would make their way out into the countryside,
carrying a small case, bag, or maybe just a blanket over their shoulder.
A number of them queued for late-afternoon buses, which would typically
take them on to the fringes of Dartmoor, usually in the Roborough and
Yelverton areas. Some owners of large properties in the countryside just
outside the city charged exorbitant rents to evacuees, and even families
who made their way to the perimeter of the moor each night were charged
for sleeping in cowsheds. The majority of these would return to Plymouth
next day, but some settled more permanently, camping in caravans or tents.
Not everybody who left the city on a temporary basis could be guaranteed

to come back safe and sound. In November 1941 one German raider was repulsed by the recently intensified barrage and therefore flew east, unloading its bombs about 15 miles away on the village of Ugborough, near Ivybridge. A bungalow was destroyed, leaving a Plymouth evacuee woman dead and eight others injured.

Strict petrol rationing did not prevent those with cars from driving out of the city and parking along the roadside or hedges, often following each other in convoy. Of those on foot the luckier ones might find a passing lorry slowing down for them to give them a lift, many having the capacity for around thirty passengers each. The grammar school at Plympton, which had been the birthplace of the eighteenth-century painter Sir Joshua Reynolds, was opened as a rest centre for trekkers. Free supper and breakfast and a blanket for the night would be supplied. A similar rest centre could be found a few miles further east at the Wesleyan church hall, Ivybridge, where lorries and buses would set down their passengers. A little closer to the city, Roborough Village Hall made provision for women and children to stay the night, while on the moorland around Roborough Down and Yelverton, some slept out in the open during the summer weeks. Others found barns and lofts in which to spend the night.

Digging for Victory – allotments on Plymouth Hoe, with the Armada Memorial and Smeaton's Tower in the background. (Derek Tait)

Yet while some people left Plymouth, others stayed where they were. One voluntary warden, the father of four children who remained in safety in their garden shelter with their mother, continued to work. When asked why he did not take the family away, he answered that this was his home, it was all he had, and that was where his job was. 'Besides, this is Plymouth's finest hour. I should hate to miss it!'

All possible space in the city that could reasonably be used to grow food was given over to suitable produce. A Corporation piggery was created in the old farm at Central Park, with the pigs being fed on edible kitchen and table waste placed in refuse bins by the public. Householders made full use of small plots attached to their homes, thus more than doubling the number of allotments already provided by the Corporation. Vegetables were not rationed during the war, a factor which probably contributed to their frequently being in short supply. Private gardens in the city which had once consisted of carefully tended areas of lawn and flowerbeds now grew potatoes, lettuces, beans and tomatoes instead. City parks, including a large area of Plymouth Hoe, were turned into allotments, where people could often be seen enthusiastically 'digging for victory'. Great efforts were made to collect paper, rags, rubber, tin, iron, steel, cooking fat and silk stockings, all of which were carefully sorted and put into separate containers in regular salvage drives organised to help the war effort. By the end of 1944 the value of materials recovered and sold by the City Engineers' and Surveyors' Departments stood at almost £200,000.

Many of the men who had worked in agriculture during peacetime had joined the services, and there was an acute shortage of agricultural labour. This prompted the formation of the Land Army, and by 1944 over 80,000 women throughout Britain, including a sizeable contingent in Plymouth and the surrounding area, were undertaking general farm work and jobs such as milking, cutting down trees and working in sawmills.

On 23 May 1943 a service was held in St Andrew's church, the first since its virtual destruction. Several hundred people turned up to attend, far more than anticipated, and police had to come and control the crowds. The charred wood, blackened and blistered masonry was removed from the interior, grass was laid where the pews had been, and borders of scarlet geraniums were arranged where the choir and clergy stalls led to the altar. A simple altar was erected under a temporary cover. From the summer of 1943 onwards, garden services were held there every Sunday evening, with the organist, Dr Harry Moreton, leading the singing as he played a small manual organ at the foot of the pulpit, which was fitted with a microphone and loudspeaker.

Land Army girls marching past the City Museum. (Derek Tait)

National League football was suspended and grass grew high on the untended pitch. Although the Plymouth Argyle stands had been bombed in April, local football was kept alive with the formation of the Plymouth City Club and the Plymouth United Club, who played games against service teams. Greyhound racing was a major attraction at Plymouth

Greyhound Stadium. Both the local daily newspapers, *Western Morning News* and *Western Evening Herald*, continued to publish six days a week, though for a while the nightly disruption meant that the *Western Morning News* had to be printed at the offices of the *Express and Echo* in Exeter until offices at Tavistock could be made available for the purpose. Production was based there until October 1944, when staff returned to the Plymouth office. Pat Twyford, who made regular journeys to Exeter by car with key editorial and mechanical staff, later recalled a 'fearful picture' of the city as he and his colleagues left 'the inferno' behind them, him driving while they looked back, 'watching that terrible glow in the sky which marked the burning city'. The *Western Evening Herald* maintained production in Frankfort Street as the work could be carried out during daytime, when raids were less likely to occur. Plymouth's Sunday newspaper, the *Western Independent*, formerly had its head offices and works in Russell Street, and when these were destroyed it opened offices at Alton Terrace for the editorial and commercial departments, while printing and publication were carried out at alternative premises in Ivybridge.

Although there were several alerts during the next few months, no major incidents took place in Plymouth until 23 November 1942. That night a raider was brought down by a Polish night-fighter directly over Plymouth. A crowd was watching a glow of fire which gradually grew in size, until it looked like a flaming cigar racing through the night sky as it circled around and then crashed in a field near the Roborough–Tamerton road. The four occupants, one wounded, climbed out unhurt and were captured.

In March 1943 the recently widowed Marina, Duchess of Kent paid a brief visit to the city as a guest of Lord and Lady Astor. In the space of a few packed hours during the morning, she toured some of the worst bombed areas; saw the War Aid Supply Department; met representatives of the Guildhall Working League, the Women's Voluntary Service and other women's organisations; and then continued to Strathmore Hall where she met voluntary workers from other bodies, and leaders of trade and commerce. In the afternoon she opened a Service Women's Hostel and canteen, and a new fire station.

A few weeks later the 29th Division of the American Army moved from Salisbury Plain to Devon and Cornwall, and took over the Seaton and Plumer Barracks at Crownhill, as well as Raglan Barracks, Devonport. For a while they were more familiar in the streets of Plymouth than the British soldiers. At the same time, in November, the United States Naval Advanced Amphibious Base which had been set up to house and train American service personnel preparing for the D-Day landings established a base at Queen Anne's Battery, Coxside, where Construction Battalions built a ship repair yard, a dry dock and three marine rail tracks for the repair and maintenance of American naval craft. The commanding officer, Captain C.F.M.S. Quimby, occupied Hamoaze House at Mount Wise. Other locations forming part of the base included Victoria Wharf, Martin's Wharf, Commercial Wharf, Baltic Wharf, Cattedown Quarry, Pomphlett Quarry, Shapter's Field, Richmond Walk, Turnchapel, Efford, Manadon, the old Stonehouse police station, Saltash Passage, the grounds of Saltram House, Edinburgh Street at Devonport, Coypool Depot at Marsh Mills, Chaddlewood, the Brickfields, and Devonport Park.

These overseas servicemen brought with them some of their customs and activities, introduced baseball to the area and formed their own local team, the Plymouth Yankees, which played on Saturday evenings at Pennycross Stadium, with gate receipts being given to local charities. In January 1944 the American soldiers opened a camp at Vicarage Road, St Budeaux, which housed forces engaged in preparations for the D–Day landings later that year.

American troops, who had arrived in Plymouth in spring 1943, helping to clear up debris in the streets. (Derek Tait)

The Americans found a ready welcome in Plymouth. Among other sights they were naturally interested to see the Mayflower Stone on the Barbican, commemorating the sailing of the *Mayflower* with the Pilgrim Fathers to America in 1620. Plymothians were most impressed by the way in which the Americans got on with a job of work without fuss. A site was chosen at Manadon Vale for a new naval hospital with 250 beds. It was built on land previously owned by an archery club by the American Construction Battalion. Within two months they had put in the foundations, built the camp from sections, nuts, bolts and equipment sent across the Atlantic, and had it fully equipped for dealing with X-rays, general and dental surgery, and orthopaedic and traumatic injuries. Arrangements were made which would enable it to double in size and capacity if there should be additional injured troops from France, and it was opened in February 1944.

By mid-1943, of the 12,000 children who had been evacuated, 8,000 had returned, thus creating a serious difficulty for the Education Authority from the point of view of accommodation and of providing sufficient teaching staff. Ninety schools had been destroyed or seriously damaged, and many secondary schools had moved to other towns. Devonport High School for Boys was evacuated to Penzance, Sutton Secondary School to St Austell, Devonport High School for Girls to Tiverton, Plymouth Girls' School to Newquay, and St Boniface College to Buckfast Abbey. Plymouth College, which was undamaged in the raids, remained at Hyde Park Corner.

Throughout 1942 the brunt of the bombing raids had fallen on Exeter, causing destruction and loss of life on a major scale. However, over the next two years Plymouth would also suffer once again. In the early hours of 14 June 1943 there was a half-hour raid on the city centre and Plympton, during which over seventy high-explosive bombs were dropped. Thirteen people were killed, and about 3,000 houses were destroyed or damaged. The death toll would probably have been much higher, had not about half the bombs failed to detonate. One of the largest came through the roof at Greenbank police headquarters, bringing a large amount of masonry crashing down, and remained on the landing of the first floor outside the magistrate's court and over the prison cells and control room without exploding. The reserve headquarters at Widey Court were brought into use on a temporary basis until after the bomb was removed and the damage made good by the new National Fire Service and firefighters from Canada.

Four of the twenty or so planes responsible for carrying out the attack were brought down. That same day, a Junkers 88 crashed in the garden of a house at Stoke which was being used as a hostel for the WRNS or Women's Royal Naval

A barrage balloon landing on the Strathmore Hotel in Eliot Street, as a crowd gathers to watch near the adjacent Bedford Hotel. (Derek Tait)

A Junkers 88, which crashed at Stoke in June 1943 with the loss of all the crew. (Derek Tait)

Service. It was the first enemy plane to meet such a fate in the city during the war. All the crew inside burnt to death, and their charred remains were buried at Weston Mill Cemetery with full Air Force honours.

One young Nazi airman was more fortunate. He had bailed out of his aeroplane, landed in Lisson Grove, Mutley Plain, and was promptly captured by Mr Doidge, a warden, who thus became the only member of the service to capture an enemy airman in the city streets during the whole war. The young man had been stricken with terror by the sound of a bomb dropping, and was seen to shudder at the flames as he was taken past a shop which was ablaze at the time. When the news was released, one small detail was expunged by the censor and not revealed to the public until after the end of the war almost two years later. In order to take the man captive, Doidge had found it necessary to remove a piece of string from his pocket, tie it firmly around the young man's wrists and lead him along the back lane by the loose end. However, it had been feared that any revelation of use of the string at the time would have led to an international outcry, and consequent exploitation by the Nazi propaganda machine, about 'binding prisoners of war'.

Two further raids on the city took place that year. On the night of 11 August the area between Laira and Devonport was attacked, with forty-one men, women and children killed, and about 160 injured. Three months later, on 16 November, bombs fell on Devonport and the Pennycross, Mannamead and Stoke area, with eighteen people killed, about sixty injured, and some forty houses completely destroyed.

Also in November Private R.L. Millett of the Royal Army Ordnance Corps, who lived in Athenaeum Street, returned home to celebrate his fiancee's twenty-first birthday. He had been taken prisoner at Hazebrouke, about 20 miles from Dunkirk, in May 1940, and had spent the next three years being held in prison camps in Germany and Poland. When he came back he told of his ill-health, treatment by doctors, and of how the Germans had established half-hourly roll calls throughout the day and night, as some of the men had been late starting their work. 'We got up laughing,' he said. 'They soon got fed up with that!' Despite endless days of hard and tedious work, monotony and poor food, Millett said that the repatriation of himself and his colleagues meant that, 'As soon as we saw once more the coast of Britain we forgot our long weekend abroad.'

After a respite of five months, what proved to be the final aerial attack on Plymouth came on 30 April 1944, when an alert sounded at 3.15 a.m. Over thirty aircraft mounted an attack, their main target being the waterfront. Eighteen people were killed and seven were seriously injured in the

HMS *Colombo*, an anti-aircraft ship, secured to a buoy in Plymouth Sound, July 1943. (Steve Johnson)

Oreston area. At the depot of the Western National Omnibus Company at Prince Rock, three fire watchers were killed, sixteen other men were seriously injured and many buses were burnt out. An Anderson shelter was hit with the loss of six lives, and a public shelter nearby was struck with a death toll of nine. Browning Road, Fisher Road and Beaumont Street at Milehouse, also suffered serious damage. Bombs landed on the Rising Sun public house, Crabtree, Laira railway sidings, the Tothill recreation ground and the Gas Company's recreation ground, leaving a huge crater but without causing any damage to vehicles caused nearby.

On 28 May, Whit Sunday, as part of the build-up to the Allied invasion of Normandy, General Montgomery came to Plymouth and addressed a meeting of American army officers at the Odeon Cinema. A week later, on 3 June, a fund-raising drive in aid of the armed forces, Salute the Soldier Week, was opened by Admiral of the Fleet, Baron Chatfield, a former First Sea Lord. In launching the appeal, he evoked the name of a local hero from long ago as he called on the city's part in the campaign to 'be worthy of its wonderful history, equal to your greatest efforts in other ways; something you will look back on with pride, that will even rouse Drake from his long sleep as the deeds of Plymouth men and women have done before.'

Later that summer Plymouth was witness to one of the last performances by one of the greatest of the wartime bandleaders. On 28 August Glenn Miller and his fifty-two-piece band flew in from Bedford to RAF Harrowbeer, Yelverton, and were taken to Plymouth. They stayed at Queen Anne's Battery, and that night they appeared at the Odeon Cinema, playing to an audience of 2,000 made up of British and American servicemen. It had been wrongly rumoured that Bing Crosby would also appear. Queues started to form more than an hour before the doors opened, and the police and military police had to form cordons to control the crowd. It would be one of Glenn Miller's final concerts before leaving for Europe where he was to plan a six-week tour. He boarded a flight for Paris on 15 December to supervise arrangements in advance, and the plane was lost over the English Channel.

Meanwhile preparations for the invasion of Europe were being made, and the US Army was practising landings on the long stretch of Slapton Sands for the occasion, while the fleet was building up in the Sound. On D-Day, 6 June 1944, the V and VII Corps of General Bradley's 1st Army, comprising some 36,000 troops, embarked from Plymouth for the Normandy landings. Three prayer services were held that day in the garden church of St Andrews. Throughout the city, when the news became public knowledge at about 9.30 a.m., it was greeted with what the papers described as 'traditional philosophical calm'. People must have grown weary of false dawns and supposed turning points in the war, but later it dawned on them that this was particularly good news, and 'a new animation of subdued optimism' was perceptible. The first vessels to leave Plymouth were 110 ships carrying the men of the United States VII Corps of the 4th Infantry Division, under the command of Rear-Admiral D.P. Moon aboard USS *Bayfield*. After joining up with more vessels and troops from Salcombe, Dartmouth and Brixham, they were among the first to land at Utah Beach. From 24 July the Vicarage Road camp was used as a receiving base for troops returning from France.

On 3 December a special ceremony was held on the Hoe, in front of the Drake Memorial, at which Commander Colonel G. Thomson called Home Guard units of the Plymouth Garrison to stand down. Over 4,000 officers and men were present. A march past was led to music from the Royal Marine Band, as the battalions who had worked unceasingly for the last five years paraded for the final time, prior to the orders of 'Stand Down' and 'Dismiss'.

Slowly but surely, certain regulations were beginning to be relaxed, and there was a growing feeling that conditions were gradually returning to normal. One of the first signs had been the withdrawal in 1943 of a regulation which required all policemen on duty to wear a respirator for half an hour every Tuesday afternoon. In December 1944, reduced lighting was once again permitted on some Plymouth streets, from Drake Circus through Cornwall, Frankfort and King Streets, to the Royal Naval Hospital, Union, and Bedford Streets, and Millbay Road. As a result the brightest patch was the Royal Cinema, where lights once again shone proudly from the upper windows with their pre-war brightness. At the same time an order making the masking of headlamps on road vehicles compulsory was rescinded.

Over the festive season, helpers at canteens and service institutions ensured that seasonal fare and programmes would be available for those in uniform to have the best possible time they could while they were far away from home and their loved ones. The Lord Mayor's Fund acted as Santa Claus to all sick or wounded servicemen and women in Plymouth hospitals, handing sums of money to the matrons to dispense as they thought fit, either giving cash or else presents of fruit, cigarettes or other treats. The Royal Sailors Rest at Devonport arranged a Christmas dinner for 200 and a party in the evening, while the St Andrew's Service Canteen laid on an afternoon tea for 300 of homemade cakes and pastries, followed by a concert and buffet supper, as well as a social dance and buffet supper on Boxing Day. Meanwhile the YMCA at Union Street prepared Christmas dinner for 200 followed by a party for 1,000 guests with tea, including sandwiches, cakes, ice cream, plus games and competitions, to be followed by another party and dance on Boxing Day. All but the most pessimistic were sure that this would almost certainly be the last wartime Christmas, and that in twelve months' time the festive season would be celebrated in much happier circumstances.

6

THE PATH
TO PEACE

In March 1945 ice creams, which had been withdrawn from sale at Gaumont cinemas in 1942, were made available once again. It was another sign that life was getting back to normal. That same month A.V. Alexander, First Lord of the Admiralty, visited the city to open a new NAAFI (Navy, Army and Air Force Institutes) Club in Lockyer Street on the site of the old Royal Hotel. After the Blitz, Plymouth had been very short of social facilities for servicemen, a point underlined by the arrival of so many more personnel in the build-up to D-Day. In his speech, he said that the people of Plymouth had taken many hard knocks, and had shown the greatest resilience throughout.

A similar tribute was paid later that week when R.A. Butler, Minister of Education, came to see for himself the immense difficulties faced in maintaining a satisfactory standard of education under such conditions. York Street School, at Fore Street in Devonport, which had facilities which were now thoroughly out of date but had remained standing in the midst of utter devastation on all sides, was described as 'the beating heart of the city'. Speaking in Central Hall that evening, he said that the teachers' record in Plymouth was unequalled in the whole country, especially with regard to evacuating children, as well as tracing and collecting those who had not left the city after the raids.

By spring 1945 the end of the war was clearly in sight. Early in April, newspaper reporters asked several people in the city from different walks of life what they would do on the approaching day when victory was declared. One housewife said she would attend a thanksgiving service and then go out to mingle with the crowds. The mother of a soldier still serving overseas insisted that she could not rejoice and celebrate until her boy returned safely from Burma. A house decorator gave his assurance that if he could continue to work he would do so, and would wait to commemorate victory until the war between all nations was over; 'How can one celebrate until the whole world is at peace again?' A solicitor's clerk thought that the occasion would be one to be observed quietly, so he would attend a service at the first opportunity and then spend the day in reflection as he did not think it would be a time for 'junketing'. A former transport worker remarked that everybody would be glad that Hitler had been thrashed, and those who had been through the fighting and experienced the bombing would be only too thankful it was over, but it would still be a sad day for all who had lost husbands or sons.

On Sunday, 29 April, the headlines on the front page of the *Western Independent* read 'Nazi State Disintegrates While Berlin Burns – Himmler Predicts Hitler's Death', and 'Berlin Is Dying In Flames: Appalling Scenes In The Last Days Of A Doomed City'. When news of Hitler's suicide in his bunker in Berlin on 30 April broke two days later, the general public reaction was guarded, even cautious, if not downright cynical. One market stallholder said he thought it was no more than a hoax, while a shopkeeper assistant suggested it was only a rumour which might have been spread in order to enable the Führer to escape from Berlin. That same day the air-raid warning system was discontinued.

According to official figures, during the war 1,172 Plymouth civilians had been killed and 3,276 injured. The city had the melancholy distinction of being the worst bombed city in Britain per capita in terms of civilian casualties. There had been 602 air-raid alerts and fifty-nine actual bombing attacks, while 3,754 houses were destroyed with a further 18,398 seriously damaged. Six hotels, eight cinemas, twenty-six schools, forty-one churches and a hundred public houses were among the buildings destroyed. The entire city centre had been obliterated except for the shells of St Andrew's church, the Guildhall, the Regent Cinema, later demolished and replaced by Littlewoods store, and the offices of the *Western Morning News*. When dress rehearsals for the pantomime at the Palace Theatre were held shortly before Christmas 1944, invitations were extended to 1,200 children. Sadly but perhaps not surprisingly, it was found that many of them were orphans. A subsequent investigation discovered that about 1,000 orphans were living in Plymouth at the time.

Germany surrendered unconditionally on 7 May, and at 3.00 p.m. on the following day, declared VE Day (Victory in Europe), an official declaration was made of an end to hostilities. Crowds gathered around the remains of the Guildhall to hear dignitaries and members of the armed forces bring the glad tidings as church bells, previously silenced except to announce an enemy invasion, rang once again throughout the city.

Bonfires were lit on the Hoe, started with timber from a damaged hut on the corner of the former balloon site near Smeaton's Tower. It was organised by the sailors, marines and merchant seamen. They were attended enthusiastically by the public and by sailors, who jubilantly threw their caps and even parts of their uniforms on the blaze as if to reinforce that the bitter and dangerous days were behind them at last, while members of the public tossed their hats, jackets and scarves the same way. The police moved all the deckchairs they could find, but not before at least thirty or so had been thrown on the flames. Some chairs were brought up from the Lido at Tinside. Dancing on the Hoe was provided by Percy Cole in his capacity as entertainments manager. He had brought some gramophone records and amplifiers along, in an early forerunner of the disco which would be a regular feature of similar parties and gatherings some two or three decades hence.

Mindful of the fact that the blackout was still in force, the fire services came to try and put the bonfire out a little prematurely. They found their way barred by the crowd, and when they tried to pour water on the fire, people defiantly uncoupled one hose and threw it on the flames. Realising that it was pointless to try and spoil everyone else's fun, the firemen retreated until about midnight when the crowds had thinned.

The two-day holiday proved a mixed blessing for Plymouth's pubs, as about 80 per cent of landlords had either sorely underestimated the demand of their customers or failed to obtain all they needed, and had to shut as they were out of beer. Once the news had got around that next day would be the one that the nation had been waiting for, at least one house sold out by 8.30 p.m. The licensee was expecting a delivery next day, but as it was an official holiday, no new supplies were forthcoming.

Mass absenteeism might have been expected when Plymouth returned to work on the following morning, but to the authorities' surprise very little was reported. People were clearly eager to get back to normal life as soon as they could. Essential services, such as buses and trains, had functioned smoothly to provide a normal service over the holiday, with employees of the Corporation's transport departments working cheerfully to ensure everything ran as expected.

Not everybody was satisfied with the victory celebrations. Later that week, over eighty customers of Hooper's Newsagents in King Street signed a protest against the lack of arrangements made on VE Day and the day following, organised by the newsagent's daughter Muriel and sent to the lord mayor. It said that the undersigned wished to express their extreme disappointment at the way in which it was 'celebrated'. There had been every opportunity, including perfect weather. Instead, 'Plymouth people wandered around forlornly on a day when our morale should have been at its peak. We felt disappointed, subdued, and thoroughly disgusted with the lack of arrangements and the leaders of our City'. People had been walking around aimlessly and looking as miserable as sin, they said, as if they had been the ones who had lost the war. At the very least, they suggested, some music and an organised sing-song could have been provided. Such criticisms were less than fair. One wonders where they had been when the crowds were watching the bonfire on the Hoe, and whether they were aware that any celebrations at such short notice were inevitably going to be of a fairly spontaneous nature.

On 11 May the Admiralty announced that lighting restrictions in coastal areas were no longer necessary for defence purposes. Full street lighting in Plymouth could be resumed, with masks on traffic lights removed, for the first time in five and a half years. But people had to wait a little longer for floodlighting and neon lights to reappear on the Hoe, as these had been destroyed during the Blitz and could not be replaced until new supplies were forthcoming. All the same, life in the city was slowly but surely resuming its old pattern. There were no public feasts on a large scale because of food rationing, only street parties with neighbours clubbing together to give the children a treat as they laid tea tables out on the pavements. As most of the able-bodied men were still on active service and had not yet returned home, nearly all those who attended were mothers and their children. Some of the parties which had begun on Tuesday were reportedly still going on Saturday.

On 13 May open-air services were held at the Garden church of the ruined St Andrew's, and at Devonport Park. The Honorary Secretary of the Plymouth Licensed Victuallers' Association recommended that its members ought to close on Sunday morning so that everybody would be able to join in the services of thanksgiving. A Thanksgiving Parade was marshalled at St Jude's by Major Wattenbach, Brigade Major of the Plymouth Garrison. It included detachments from all the armed services, Civil Defence, and voluntary youth organisations, with six bands playing, and over 3,000 men and women taking part.

On the evening of 17 May, two Royal Navy destroyers, HMS *Bulldog* and HMS *Narborough*, sailed into Plymouth Sound. They were escorting six German minesweepers and two German patrol craft, each flying the British white ensign, all having been captured in the English Channel near Guernsey. As they had sailed through Cawsand Bay, they were stopped

Crowds gathering around the Guildhall during VE Day celebrations in May 1945. (Derek Tait)

for two senior naval officers, Commander R.W.J. Martin and Lieutenant-Commander Harvey, accompanied by a contingent of Royal Marines with bayonets drawn, to board the vessel and accept the surrender of the German commander, before new orders were issued to the German crews and the ships fell into line for the final part of their journey. As they entered the Sound, crowds were lining the Hoe to watch. The trawlers were taken to Millbay Docks and remained there under guard, as the men were moved to the Royal Citadel.

On 26 May the Lord Mayor of London, Sir Frank Alexander, opened the Plymouth Royal and Merchant Navies Week at a ceremony in the Abbey Hall, with the objective of raising £15,000 for the Royal and Merchant Navies. At the opening ceremony he began his address by regretting that the city had no Guildhall in which they could receive the

Lord Mayor of London. During the morning he and the Lord Mayor of Plymouth had been to view the display sites in Plymouth together, visiting a German U-Boat, an exhibition staged at the City Museum of naval and RAF equipment used regularly during the war, including photographs and films, and a collection of landing-craft engines at Mumford's Abbey Garage, where over 200 men and women had been hard at work for the last six years overhauling, rebuilding and testing thousands of engines for landing-craft, barges and assault vessels. They had also enjoyed a short journey from Mayflower Steps in a full-scale replica of the *Golden Hind*. Later that day, at a luncheon at the Grand Hotel he remarked that their relief at the end of war in Europe was tempered with a sense of urgency of things yet to be done, and they still had 'a savage and brutal foe to overcome.' The day finished with the Lord Mayor of London taking the salute at a tattoo in the Royal Citadel.

That same day the German U-boat U-1023 arrived at Plymouth, with a British crew on board. The captain had surrendered at Portland naval base, and it was visiting various ports along the south coast in turn, open to the public in order to raise funds for the King George's Fund for Sailors. While at Plymouth it was moored in Millbay Docks and remained on public display for eight days, until 3 June. Donations were encouraged although there was no admission charge.

In addition to the exhibitions, other fund-raising activities taking place during the week included functions at service establishments, and a crossword puzzle competition with prizes, for which 10,600 entries were received. Admission to everything was free but patrons were reminded to 'Say thanks by giving' to the King George's Fund for Sailors.

For Plymouth, as for the rest of the country, life was gradually returning to normal. On 13 June public pleasure boat trips, suspended at the outbreak of war, started once again in the Hamoaze. The *Swift* sailed from Phoenix Wharf to the Royal Albert Bridge, and the *Lively* was put on as a relief boat, as about 150 passengers made the journey. Six days later *Drina*, a Royal Mail Lines' passenger liner, landed passengers at Plymouth. The first liner to call at the city for five and a half years, she had taken sixteen days to cross from Argentina. On board she was carrying twenty-five passengers and a cargo of 7,000 tons of meat bound for British troops in Germany.

On 1 July HMAS *Australia*, the flagship of the Australian Royal Navy, arrived at Devonport Dockyard for a refit and repair. A heavy cruiser of 10,000 tons, she was the largest ship in the Royal Australian Navy, she had seen action at Dakar, the Battle of Coral Sea, Gudalcanal, and in the initial assault on the Philippines. At the Battle of Leyte in October 1944 she was hit by a Japanese bomber. The crew of 700 was entertained, with tickets for the cinemas, shows at the Palace Theatre, and special dances being arranged on two evenings at the NAAFI Club.

Double Summer Time came to an end on 14 July 1945, and clocks were put back one hour. On 2 August 1945 Plymouth was the scene of a meeting between King George VI and Harry S. Truman, aboard HMS *Renown*, moored in Plymouth Sound. Truman, who had become President of the United States on the sudden death of President Franklin D. Roosevelt in April, had been one of 'the big three' allied heads of state attending the Potsdam Conference, the others being Stalin and Churchill, the latter replaced by Clement Attlee after the Labour party's victory in the general election. Truman broke his journey home, and flew from Berlin to Harrowbeer Aerodrome at Yelverton, from where he was driven into Plymouth to board the US cruiser *Augusta*, awaiting him in the Sound. The king had travelled by train from London to Millbay Docks, where a barge was ready to take him to the *Renown*. Several thousand eager Plymothians had turned out to welcome the President, a few of them even hoping to thank him for American support in person, but left having seen nothing. The initial plan was for him to see the route between Mutley Plain and Millbay, giving him a close view of the war damage. However, it had been changed at the last moment, and even the police were unaware of the exact plan. For a few hours, it appeared that the President, shielded by his military police, was even more closely guarded than the king. Only a few selected representatives from the press were allowed within close range of him, as he went direct from Greenbank and Friary Bridge to Victoria Wharves and the United States naval base embarkation points. There was major disappointment that he saw very little, if anything, of the blitzed city centre, and the press claimed that as far as the public were concerned, the visit was 'a fiasco'.

Despite this, within less than a fortnight, there would be genuine cause to celebrate. Following unconditional surrender by Japan, the war was finally over. VJ Day (Victory in Japan) was celebrated on 15 August in Plymouth by official bonfires on the Hoe, Devonport Park and Central Park. Those which had been prepared on the Hoe were lit a day earlier by certain people who could not wait. Mindful of the fact that so many deck chairs had been taken for the fire three months earlier, the authorities did their best to try and remove them to safety. Nevertheless they had not bargained for people going to such extraordinary efforts to remove park benches; even those embedded in the ground with concrete were not safe from crowds eager to keep the fire ablaze. There was considerable official annoyance at such

A street party celebrating VJ Day (Victory in Japan), to mark the end of hostilities in August 1945. (Derek Tait)

wanton vandalism. About thirty benches were removed altogether, at a cost of £300, and it was remarked that the Hoe would look very inhospitable with nowhere to sit in comfort until they could be replaced – from public funds. Also used to light the fires were a pole which had been erected for a loudspeaker to provide music for al fresco dancing the following evening, articles of uniform, an accordion, a cafe sign, trestle tables and a handcart. Corporation workmen had to spend much of the day clearing up the debris and rebuilding the bonfires.

That night and into the small hours, as almost 60,000 gathered on the Hoe to watch fires blaze and rockets in the sky, a civilian band marched through the streets blowing bugles, supplemented with makeshift cymbals removed from the City Engineer's pig-food bins. One bin was used as a football, until it rolled under a police car, which was brought to a standstill before the driver continued good-humouredly on his way. Staff from an upper window in the main post office in Tavistock Road showered ticker tape onto the crowds below, while girls from WAAF hostels, still in their pyjamas with uniform coats hastily thrown on top, stormed cars as they begged for lifts into the city centre to join in the celebrations. At 3.00 a.m. a car was seen parked across the road in Princess Square as naval officers in pyjamas and dressing gowns leant over it drinking beer. HMS *Renown* and other ships of the fleet provided a large firework display in the Sound, while at Mount Batten a dance band played for a party attended by Wrens, naval ratings, other servicemen and women and civilians who all joined in enthusiastically to favourites like 'The Lambeth Walk' and 'Hokey Cokey'.

Away from the good-tempered if sometimes understandably a little overenthusiastic crowds, some people celebrated on their own. One sailor in a lonely street was observed, it was noted, 'singing aloud in his felicity but finding it difficult to harmonise the movements of his legs with the rhythm of his song'.

Now that the conflict was over, a certain amount of gradual dismantling and orderly tidying up still remained to be done. Later that autumn, the United States army camp at Vicarage Road was decommissioned, and the remainder of the United States Naval Advanced Amphibious Base was closed as its personnel returned across the Atlantic.

Despite war-weariness Plymouth could look forward to peacetime with optimism, especially as a bold innovative plan had already been produced for the future of the city. In April 1944 the Plymouth City Council had held a special meeting to discuss the constitution of the new Reconstruction Committee. The result, the document 'Plan for Plymouth', was the joint work of James Paton Watson, the City Engineer, and Professor Patrick

Abercrombie of London University. The latter, who was already working on a reconstruction plan for Greater London, had been involved at the personal request of Lord Astor and the Emergency Committee. It was approved in principle by the Council in August 1944. Lord Astor would have been a natural choice of chairman of the Reconstruction Committee being set up to oversee implementation of the plan. However, he had worked unremittingly throughout the war years as lord mayor, his health was not good, and he wanted to retire from public life. His term of office as mayor expired in November 1944, and he was succeeded by Alderman H.G. Mason, a Labour member of the council.

Lord Astor knew that the political tide was moving strongly towards Labour, locally as well as nationally. It was evident to him and many others that if his wife contested the seat again in the forthcoming general election she would be heavily and humiliatingly defeated even though she had held it for over twenty-five years. This was partly because of the general desire for a new beginning after years of Conservative-led National government, and partly because, despite her high profile and energetic service in Plymouth during the war, her maverick behaviour, particularly some of her anti-Catholic and anti-Communist statements, had made her something of a liability. Without consulting her, he advised the Sutton Constituency Party that she would not stand again for parliament. Though she was initially angry with him, he was proved right when her successor as Conservative candidate was heavily defeated in the election of July 1945, a contest which saw the Conservative party under Churchill emphatically rejected when Labour came to power with an overall majority of 145 seats. All three Plymouth seats returned Labour members for the first time, with large swings and safe majorities. In Devonport the former minister Leslie Hore-Belisha, standing again as a Liberal National, was ousted by another Plymouth-born man, Michael Foot, whose father Isaac was a former Liberal Member of Parliament for Bodmin and was now the city's lord mayor. In Sutton, Lucy Middleton likewise triumphed over her Conservative rival, while in Drake, the only one which had ever previously returned a Labour member to Westminster, during the parliament of 1929–31, the victorious candidate was Bert Medland, who had served as lord mayor in 1935–36.

Even before the war, the city had urgently required major redevelopment. The shopping centre had expanded out of all proportion to its narrow streets, and the Civic Centre was too small for the administration workforce needed. Slum clearance and rehousing schemes had barely kept pace with the rapidly expanding population's needs, and an unchecked sprawl was threatening to erode parts of the surrounding countryside. War damage provided the city with an opportunity to create something positive from the ashes, rather than piecemeal renovation. To quote W. Best Harris, Plymouth City Librarian from 1947 to 1974 and distinguished local historian writing some years later, 'the vast destruction which had been wrought on people and property was used as a spur to inspire the need to recreate the city.' In April 1941, during the worst of the Blitz, James Paton Watson had told a reporter from the press as they stood viewing the damage from what remained of the Guildhall that in peacetime he foresaw a great modern city which would rival Copenhagen, Venice and Stockholm. Plymouth would be rebuilt with straight roads to ease traffic congestion, separated by lawns planted out with flowers and trees, and other amenities, as well as saving the older buildings which had not been completely demolished.

The 'Plan for Plymouth' also looked forward to the creation of what it, like Watson, called, 'a great modern city'. It was to be a place suitable for people to live and work in, respecting and safeguarding its links with the historic past while preparing for a prosperous future. It argued that the centre of Plymouth was the commercial hub, and initial rebuilding work should be concentrated in that area. A deliberate intention was made not to reinstate what had been a large shopping centre in Devonport based on Fore Street, as the dockyard needed room to expand. Some of Devonport's prouder residents, particularly those who could still recall the opposition to amalgamation in 1914, must have felt that this heralded a further erosion of its facilities and status. The city of Plymouth had to function as a naval dockyard, a naval and military centre, a shopping centre for a wide area, a light industrial centre, a port for sea and air, and a fishing port as well as a residential area.

A government committee had recommended that legislation should be introduced permitting a local authority to declare war damage and obsolete areas 'Reconstruction Areas', with powers of acquisition at 1939 values. The area south and west of the Great Western Railway line from Weston Mill Creek to North Road Station, bounded by North Road, Clifton Place, Greenbank and Tothill Roads and then to the River Plym, would be designated thus. Areas would be set aside for industrial development in the Millbay-Stonehouse district between Union Street, West Hoe Road, Millbay Docks and the Royal Marine Barracks and also in the zone between Sutton Harbour and Prince Rock.

During the Blitz the headmistress of a local girls' school had posted a wooden sign saying *Resurgam* ('I shall rise again') over the door of

St Andrew's church, as a defiant emblem of the city's wartime spirit in the face of such adversity. Ever since then the entrance of the building has been known as the Resurgam door, and a granite plaque with the word engraved is now permanently affixed above. Plymouth would indeed rise again, like a phoenix from the ashes.

BIBLIOGRAPHY

PRIMARY SOURCES

Plymouth and West Devon Record Office
PWDRO 1561/CD/CI/21: Correspondence relating to homeless persons
PWDRO 689/7: Correspondence between R.A.J. Walling and his son R.V. Walling

BOOKS

Bracken, C.W., *A History of Plymouth and her Neighbours* (Wakefield: SR Publishers, first published 1931, n.e. 1970).

Clamp, Arthur, *The Story of Mount Batten, Plymouth* (published by the author, n.d.).

Foot, Michael, presented by Alison Highet, *Isaac Foot: A Westcountry Boy – Apostle of England* (London: Politico's, 2006).

Fort, Adrian, *Nancy: The Story of Lady Astor* (London: Jonathan Cape, 2012).

Gill, Crispin, *Plymouth, A New History* (Tiverton: Devon Books, 1993).

Robinson, Chris, *A History of Devonport* (Plymouth: Pen & Ink, 2010).

Savignon, André, *With Plymouth Through Fire: A documentary narrative* (St Erth: Chenhalls, 1968).

Scrivener, Keith, *Plymouth at War: A pictorial account, 1939–45* (Runcorn: Archive Publications, with *Plymouth Evening Herald*, 1989).

Sykes, Christopher, *Nancy: The Life of Lady Astor* (London: Harper & Row, 1972).

Tait, Derek, *Plymouth at War* (Stroud: Tempus, 2006).

Twyford, H.P., *It Came to Our Door: The Story of Plymouth Throughout the Second World War* (Plymouth: Underhill, first published 1945, n.e. 1975).

Van der Kiste, John, *Plymouth: History and Guide* (Stroud: The History Press, 2009).

Walling, R.A.J., *The Story of Plymouth* (London: Westaway, 1950).

Wasley, Gerald, *Devon at War, 1939–1945* (Tiverton: Devon Books, 1994).

Wasley, Gerald, *Devon in the Great War, 1914–1918* (Tiverton: Devon Books, 2000).

Wasley, Gerald, *Plymouth: A Shattered City: The Story of Hitler's Attack on Plymouth and its People 1939–45* (Tiverton: Halsgrove, 2004).

NEWSPAPERS

The Times   *Western Evening Herald*
Western Morning News   *Western Independent*

INTERNET

Brian Moseley's Encyclopedia of Plymouth History, Plymouth Data website
   www.plymouthdata.info

INDEX

Also from The History Press

DEVON

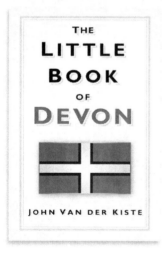
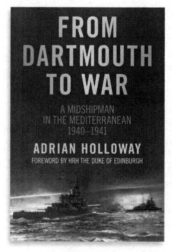
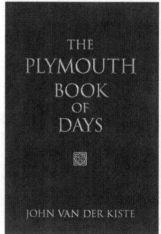

Find these titles and more at
www.thehistorypress.co.uk

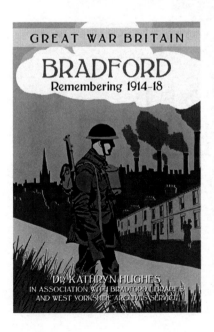

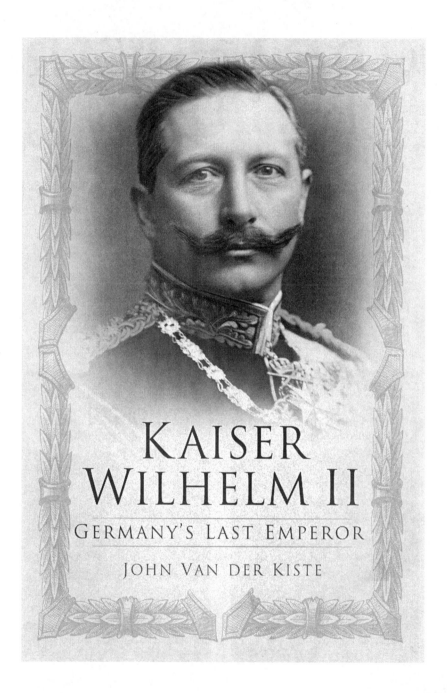

Also from The History Press

BACK TO
SCHOOL

The
History
Press

Lightning Source UK Ltd.
Milton Keynes UK
UKOW04f1525190314

228438UK00001B/1/P